Diamond Dividends
Creative Strategies to Profit Through Fantasy Baseball

MARIO MERGOLA

Copyright © 2017 Mario Mergola

All rights reserved. This book or any portion thereof may not be reproduced or used in any manner whatsoever without the express written permission of the publisher except for the use of brief quotations in a book review.

Although every precaution has been taken to verify the accuracy of the information contained herein, the author and publisher assume no responsibility for any errors or omissions. No liability is assumed for damages that may result from the use of information contained within.

ISBN: 0-9987931-0-8
ISBN-13: 978-0-9987931-0-8

DEDICATION

To Tina, Hayley, and Noelle

The only loves in my life more special to me than baseball

CONTENTS

	Acknowledgments	I
1	Every New Beginning Comes From…	1
2	Premarket Trading	4
3	The World's Series	11
4	The Albers Effect	17
5	Minimum Reasonable Expectations	23
6	Maximum Exposure	30
7	You are on the Clock	37
8	Painting the Big Picture	46
9	Win the Daily Fantasy Sprints	57
10	Shifting the Paradigm	63
11	Beginning's End	67
	Appendix I – Top 500 Player Projections	73
	Appendix II – Additional Access	104

ACKNOWLEDGMENTS

From the love and support of my wife, children, mom, dad, sister, grandparents, and friends, to the readers who have dedicated their time to taking in the content I have put out into the world, everyone has helped me turn this dream into a reality. From the bottom of my heart, thank you. I do, however, want to call special attention to those who directly aided in the creation of this book.

Brian Fitzsimmons – On an August night in South Carolina, I reached out to one of my closest friends. I had no idea what to expect, nor what I wanted, but I called Brian and talked for more than an hour about writing. He is the friend who reviewed the first sports post I had written, a published author – *Celtic Pride: How Coach Kevin Boyle Took St. Patrick to the Top of High School Basketball* – and the writer who never stopped helping me hone my craft. After the call, he referred me to Thomas Fitzgerald.

Thomas Fitzgerald – I had written in a freelance capacity at a number of sites, but XN Sports catapulted my career. Tom – the website's editor and co-founder – allowed me take the reins of my own words, enhance my strengths, and expand my reach. He believed in my writing and insight, allowed me to host his website's podcast, helped me become a regular weekly on-air guest on a radio show, and was instrumental as both a friend and advisor during the creation of Sporfolio – where Tom serves as the lead NHL writer.

Sandy Cerami – To say that this book would not exist without Sandy would be a massive understatement. The idea to create – let alone, pursue – Sporfolio stemmed entirely from his mind, and the countless hours of advice, direct suggestions, and the resolve that I "*will* write a book" is exactly why these pages exist. I often refer to Sandy as my "mentor" or "most-trusted business friend," but those tags downplay his importance. He is an inspiration on every level.

My wife, Tina – I lied. I needed to include one family member in my acknowledgements because she is the one who held my hand throughout this journey. Support and belief in me were second-nature for my 'partner-in-crime,' but Tina's efforts to always put me in a position to succeed is why this dream came true.

1 EVERY NEW BEGINNING COMES FROM…

Some cross between a scream and an unintelligible set of words from the English language left my mouth. A yelp, perhaps. And I left the ground.

Scenarios of all sorts had been running through my mind. Different options. Potential outcomes. None of which involved Rajai Davis – with 55 *career* regular season home runs spanning eleven years – sending a pitch thrown by Aroldis Chapman over the fence.

The scream-yelp was one of elation. Amazement. Everything that I – and anyone who would read a book about baseball – love about America's pastime had just unfolded on the most dramatic stage imaginable.

I wanted to cry. My vision blurred. Out of the corner of my wet eyes, I noticed a smile fill my wife's face. She had seen me distraught over the previous few weeks as the NFL season – something that had provided nothing but joy and success for me both personally and professionally – began to fail me. This was, in the realm of sports, the first time she had seen me emit pure joy in far too long.

Quickly, she had realized that my outburst was in direct

opposition of what-had-become 'The Story of 2016.' That is, the Chicago Cubs were about to break their century-long World Series drought, and I was actively rooting against it. Passionately, as my actions would confirm.

Without following the sport of baseball, she knew the importance of the moment. It was impossible to escape the storyline for anyone within earshot of a news outlet. Not necessarily one that focuses on sports. She pressed me for a reason, curious as to how her husband – a baseball romantic – was hoping for a fan base to continue its suffering.

That's exactly *why* I wanted the Cubs to lose. The baseball romantic inside of me wants the story. I craved it. I needed more. I didn't particularly care if it were Chicago, Cleveland, or any other city with something more on the line than a piece of hardware. I was born and raised believing that magic exists in sports. I believed in the curse.

Twitter had always been a fantastic mechanism for connecting with people across all walks of life – celebrities engaging with fans, athletes publicly conversing with one another, etc. – but it took on another lifeform on a Wednesday night in early November. Twitter became the stadium in which we sat while observing one of the greatest sporting events in history.

Hyperbole didn't stand a chance against Game 7 of the 2016 World Series.

Everyone was a fan of something. Everyone was an expert. Everyone had an opinion. Most importantly, everyone was watching and everyone was talking exclusively about baseball.

Electricity carried over into Thursday. The majority of random baseball fans were "just happy to see the Cubs finally win" – it should not be surprising that this irked me to no end, but my anger subsided when I saw a woman dressed head-to-toe in Cubs gear and assumed that she hadn't bought the apparel overnight.

Those who had watched more than ten innings of baseball in 2016 were baffled by the managerial decisions of Joe Madden over the previous few days. And then there were the lifelong fans of this beautiful sport still trying to wrap their collective heads around what we just witnessed. It was easy for the media to *tell* people that history was being made. It was another to watch it unfold step-by-step. It is what led to an email from a diehard baseball fan, great friend, and one of the best sports minds I know. Aptly, the subject was: Curse Breaker Theories.

I needed something. An answer. An explanation. A catalyst as to *why* it finally happened. I know and acknowledge that this Cubs team is better than any that the franchise has fielded in the last century. That never mattered before. Why did it matter now?

It took a moment of complete silence for it to hit me. A time in which only ambient sound from my surroundings filtered through my ears. Not a driving rainstorm, but not a distraction, either. Just a break in the action. A pause. A chance to reset.

The Chicago Cubs had the same benefit. They received the same breaking point. The ability to reset a game before its conclusion. The rain delay – short as it may have ended up – stopped the momentum moving against the Cubs and gave Chicago the chance to regain it. Luck? Perhaps.

Divine intervention? For some, baseball *is* a religion.

I was content. I found my answer. My peace. My acceptance of *how* the last great curse in baseball was broken. I needed to reflect in order to accept this and move forward. Finally, I could.

Now, a different question filled my mind:

What could Major League Baseball possibly do for an encore?

2 PREMARKET TRADING

I used to force myself to wait. Despite bursting with excitement for a new baseball season enveloping me as quickly as the last football season ended, I still created some self-imposed cutoff point. I would simply not allow myself to begin preparations for baseball season until I could decompress from recent NFL action. Usually, I would wait for my seasonal allergies to kick in. Then, I would know I was ready.

I stopped this silly routine. I live for this stuff. Baseball is in my blood and there is an unquenchable thirst to 'solve' it. Certainly, delaying gratification had its perks, but so did instant gratification. As soon as I let myself rekindle a relationship that had taken a hiatus lasting nearly four months, I felt the immediate connection.

My spreadsheets took only a fraction of the time to update. My projections from last year needed only slight tweaking – with the exception of home runs, which were given a full overhaul – and the content began to flow.

A combination of unparalleled momentum gained from 2016 and sheer excitement for whatever 2017 will bring powered me forward. Perhaps this new Major League Baseball season *can't* compete with the last one. But it can undoubtedly continue enhancing our experience as analysts, prognosticators and, most importantly, fans.

Every year, we are tasked with deciphering just how valuable preseason games are for projecting future success. There have been studies – specifically, focusing on pitchers – but they are often limited to measurable attributes. Certainly, position battles have merit, as they directly impact an eventual starting lineup, but we don't need to follow the games as much as the news, in this regard.

Ultimately, almost everything that is derived from preseason statistics fails to track the one element that matters most: perceived value.

Even if everyone in a fantasy league unilaterally decides to discount the events of late February and March, there is bound to be one owner who goes rogue. This is where the danger lies. The 'sleeper' we target may produce a killer Spring Training and, for no reason other than an outstanding set of statistics in *exhibition games*, we may no longer be able to afford said player. This threatens to negate the hard work we already put into our preparation.

Sometimes, a player's rising value will be unavoidable. Savvy fantasy owners will have already been tracking this athlete and need nothing more than to see him on an actual baseball field before buying in. We can accept this as long as we are aware of the player's *starting* point.

We should already have projections in place – if you are reading this, you have access to mine in Appendix I, as well. These will form our baseline set. They will change based on an increase or decrease to expected playing time, and these adjustments are the single-most – and only – important takeaway from on-field preseason action. We *can* allow ourselves to move a player up-or-down the ranks due to a respective increase or decrease in playing time. But, this is a function of direct news, not direct observations.

As soon as a batter hits a home run or pitcher strikes out the side during a preseason game, his value goes up. Every action he takes – despite the otherwise meaningless nature of the games for the established Major League starter – will influence the perception of this player, and his cost will vary continuously. It is imperative that we take note of the players that will undergo this phenomenon. As soon as they reach a relative price point that is greater than we were *originally* intending to play, we should move away. Let someone else pay the premium.

Unfortunately, the players who will most likely be impacted by such a meteoric rise will be the ones who were actually *undervalued* by most in the beginning. Small sample sizes and more rumors than facts will have led to a diminished representation of rookies or second-year players who have yet to secure a foothold with the Major League club. Potential fantasy owners will acknowledge that, in time, these players will produce, but they were otherwise unaware that the 'time' had arrived. A hot Spring Training will make believers out of doubters and force our hand.

Kris Bryant was a perfect example of this in his 2015 rookie campaign. The young superstar was highly touted as one of the game's best prospects and a hitter who would immediately make an impact in fantasy lineups.

Before stepping onto a field in Spring Training, Bryant's value was based entirely on speculation. At the time, I was already the fantasy owner most willing to pay the highest price. No one came close to my bids in auction leagues, and I guaranteed a friend of mine that taking Bryant in the tenth round of a keeper league – drafting early in the preseason – was not only the right move, but one that should have happened at least a half hour earlier.

Then, Kris Bryant *did* step on a field. And his price never stopped rising.

In 14 games – *fourteen games* – Bryant slugged nine home runs, scored 14 runs, and racked up 17 hits en route to a robust .425 batting average. The immeasurable statistic? The countless fantasy owners he won over by heroics in March.

I no longer would get Bryant at a discount, so I had a decision to make. Either I let him go to another fantasy owner or I up my ante. The former would be the result of careful planning and sticking to a system where emotions were checked at the door. I chose the latter.

Kris Bryant would now cost me more than I budgeted – either in an auction or a snake draft, where I had to consider him with one of my first three picks. But, I also knew that the increase from my baseline – essentially, the fifth round – was extremely slight compared to the adjustments other owners would need to make – possibly, the tenth round. They were surely going to get nervous moving Bryant so violently up their draft boards and, when all the chips were eventually on the table, it would be clear that I was not bluffing.

It worked. But, it only worked because my baseline was established beforehand and the rise of Bryant – meteoric as it was – moved him from 'severely undervalued' to 'slightly overvalued.' I could afford to pay the small premium to land the eventual Rookie of the Year.

Stark contrasts to Kris Bryant's rightfully inflated value can be found in nearly every other Spring Training throughout history. Bryant is actually the exception. Someone like Juan Nicasio in 2016 is the rule.

Nicasio exploded onto draft boards after posting 24 strikeouts in only 15 Spring Training innings. His zero earned runs also helped boost his stock.

The numbers were eye-popping. Unbelievable, really. So, no one actually believed them. At least, at first.

Searching for answers, a narrative was attached to Nicasio. He had been drafted and developed by the Colorado Rockies and, like so many other pitchers throwing in the thin air of Denver, struggled in the early portion of his career. But, he wasn't in Colorado, anymore. He was now with the Pirates and pitching coach Ray Searage, who just-so-happened to be the toast-of-the-town among non-managers around Major League Baseball. It didn't matter that Nicasio actually pitched for the Dodgers the year before. His story was now written. And people began bidding as if it were etched in stone.

I couldn't. I am a firm believer that *attempting* to provide a narrative to explain the unexplainable confirms that it has no validity. If I need to justify my actions, then they didn't speak loud enough, on their own.

Nicasio was completely off my list prior to his outstanding Spring Training. His baseline was as low as possible – essentially, not worth owning. But, his performances were so stellar that he did, indeed, earn a spot in the Pirates' starting rotation. The increase of guaranteed playing time – at least, in April – was enough to move him onto the fringes of my radar. Now, I would only own Nicasio if he remained a discount.

I was willingly outbid by other fantasy owners in nearly every one of my leagues when Nicasio's name – or projected round – appeared. My emotional side worried that I had made a mistake. The analytical side was pleased to see other names fall to me.

Nicasio did carry his ridiculous strikeout rate into the regular season, fanning 138 batters in only 118 innings. But, he did pitch *only 118 innings* on the season. 12 starts – four quality starts – a 4.50 ERA, and a major bullet dodged by fantasy owners who refused to be swayed by Nicasio's spring.

Surely, there will be names that emerge onto people's draft boards that were previously complete unknowns. And there will be late-round targets whose stock rises so quickly that it will force us to make critical decisions on-the-fly. As long as we know where these players originally ranked, we can justify or decline paying the price.

The following is a list of player whose value I expect to increase over the course of Spring Training, and for whom I would be willing to pay the inflated price:

Aaron Judge – Incredible power whose home runs will 'wow' fans and fantasy owners, alike. His moonshots won't make highlight reels because of their frequency, but rather the possibility that they may actually land on the moon. This opens eyes. But, we want to see his playing time guaranteed out of Spring Training and, if this ends up being the case, I will pay more to draft him.

Hunter Renfroe – Another power bat, but one who is already popular enough to potentially be out-of-reach. Renfroe has a starting position in the Padres' lineup, so we actually want him to *underwhelm* in Spring Training. We can increase our bids slightly if he tears the cover off the ball, but I would prefer if he has a modest campaign.

Ryon Healy – Copy-and-paste everything I just wrote for Hunter Renfroe and assign it to Ryon Healy. Power hitter. Slotted in the starting lineup. And some Major League Baseball experience under his belt. The man has power and, if he displays too much of it, might surpass our buying price.

Tyler Glasnow – Tyler Glasnow's strikeout potential is absurd, but his control will continue to be an issue until he can harness it. This may be one of the rare instances where we *do* want to see some improvement in exhibition games, where Glasnow could experiment. I'll be watching his walk rate more than his strikeout totals, but the latter tends to drive the boat.

Cody Bellinger – Like Renfroe and Healy, it may be too late to get a discount on Cody Bellinger. Then again, there is inherent risk that the potential Gold Glove first baseman will need to wait for an opening in Los Angeles. Thankfully, Bellinger's athleticism allows for multi-position eligibility when he does get the call. We will need Bellinger to strike the perfect balance between convincing the Dodgers to use his bat now while suppressing the excitement of the fantasy baseball community.

Chris Devenski – We have something here. We want to keep it to ourselves. But, we also want our assets to appreciate in value. Help us, Houston, just do so discreetly. Chris Devenski quietly put together an outstanding rookie campaign in 2016, posting a 2.16 ERA with nearly one-strikeout-per-inning. The term 'quietly' comes into play because Devenski spent almost the entire season pitching out of the bullpen, severely limiting his fantasy baseball production. But, his actual on-field numbers were stellar enough for him to finish fourth in American League Rookie of the Year voting. Ideally, drafting early in the preseason could lead to a speculative pick of Devenski in hopes that he wins a rotation spot but, if he gets tabbed as one of the Astros' starting pitchers entering the regular season, expect his price tag to soar.

3 THE WORLD'S SERIES

The decision to finally allow myself to be fully immersed in baseball preparation while snow billowed from the sky was made a bit easier by an event scheduled in March of 2017. One that has received its share of criticism and support, alike.

Shortly after the start of Spring Training, I, along with baseball fans around the world, would be treated to actual, competitive games in the form of the World Baseball Classic – the fourth installment. Granted, these games are also of the exhibition variety, but they are far from meaningless. However important the element of international pride proves to be during this preseason tournament, the reality of a bond tied to a baseball field cannot be denied.

During the 'typical' Spring Training game, an emphasis is placed on establishing a routine without exposing oneself to injury. It is a time to experiment within the bounds of both the game and a body's limitation. When an organization feels that its investment has completed the necessary requirements, it promptly removes said asset from the field and replaces it with a less valuable one. The words may never be spoken, but the message is clear: don't push it.

No such comment would resonate in a locker room filled with athletes ready to *compete*. Certainly, the trophy that the winning team would hoist is nothing compared to the elation gained from winning the World Series, but there is a clear goal and objective that a group of ballplayers are trying to accomplish together. Ballplayers who willingly *chose* to forego the safety of Spring Training.

As always, our job is to gain an advantage through their actions.

Whatever weight we assign to preseason statistics, we need to acknowledge that the World Baseball Classic is, by comparison, more impactful. On a case-by-case basis, we may ultimately dismiss a player's numbers in March, whether they were accumulated against the Brewers' split-squad defense or Canada's national team, but the latter was likely more important because there was an emphasis placed on winning.

Since we won't be able to follow the Major League Baseball regular season for another month after Spring Training starts, the World Baseball Classic will act as a viable bridge. Both for our baseball needs and our fantasy draft preparations.

Unfortunately, the blanket statement that gives a boost to World Baseball Classic games over those in Spring Training is not only obvious, but tricky to quantify. It hardly needs to be stated that a player who explodes on the international stage may see his value rise to a point where he can no longer be targeted. And there are dozens of fantasy-relevant athletes who will partake in this event. We don't need to list all of them since they are all subject to the same perception shift based on how the at-bats, pitches, and games unfold. Except, of course, those who are trying to rebound from a comparatively 'down' 2016 campaign.

Tampa Bay's Chris Archer is *the* ideal player to watch during the World Baseball Classic. After his third consecutive season in which he posted earned run averages of exactly 3.22 or 3.23, Archer stumbled to the tune of a 4.02 ERA in 2016. He did not necessarily collapse, but the encore to a 2015 All-Star appearance was a cut below what his fantasy owners expected.

At face value, Archer anchoring the pitching staff for the United States' national team affords fans an early look at how the right-handed pitcher plans to rebound in 2016. But, as previously stated, this is true for any player in the World Baseball Classic. Whether or not he is coming off a bad season, don't we want our potential targets to show us that our investment in them will be rewarded?

Outside the obvious desire to see encouraging statistics, do we have a cutoff point where we no longer want Archer to pitch? Does he need to continually build off previous outings in order to hone his craft right before the start of the season, or do we want the United States to end their run quickly so that Archer can return to his Major League club? For pitchers, it is impossible to shake the fear that the extra tax on one's arm will come back to haunt us. But, is this cost worth paying if it appears to right the ship?

We may not be able to answer every rhetorical question we have asked ourselves, but we can find alternate ways to view this potential 'problem.'

Unless we had some ulterior motive to *want* Archer to fail – such as resentment for another owner in a fantasy league or simply being a fan of a team that shares the division with the Rays – it would be irrational to root for anything other than Archer to succeed in March. Even if the numbers won't carry over to the regular season, the confidence *could*. And a bad showing by Archer may not sink him, but it certainly won't help. Therefore, the only real consideration is the impact of additional 'important' pitches thrown prior to the start of the regular season.

Since we clearly won't be privy to inside information regarding Archer's eventual health, we can watch the warning signs from the outside. Essentially, the Tampa Bay Rays have no reason to do anything with Archer other than handing him the ball every fifth day. There is no value in tweaking the system and there is absolutely no apparent reason to consider trading him. Archer is a young, established pitcher with the makeup of a potential 'ace' for years to come. But, that is the Chris Archer *we* see. And the Rays are generally creative when tasked with fitting a round peg into a square hole, especially when the peg is quietly altered.

Chris Archer currently fits on the Rays' roster. Not only is he still an excellent on-field presence – just look at his strikeout rate – but he is an unquestioned clubhouse leader. A student of the game. A good example.

Still, if the right deal is thrown in Tampa Bay's direction, would the front office entertain it? More importantly, what would push the Rays out of the 'listening' business and into the deal-making one? Probably, an internal realization that Archer is, indeed, wearing down.

We cannot make any outward plays involving Archer until the season begins and the opportunity presents itself. But, we can continually monitor the situation and act accordingly. Tampa Bay *will* tip its proverbial hand.

Following Archer's season into the summer months will be easy enough. His current draft position suggests fair value, and we can justify owning the pitcher as long as the price is right. We can also let him walk away. For now.

By the time July rolls around, as long as Archer is healthy, he will be a target of playoff-bound teams. Pay close attention. We want to mirror the actions of the Tampa Bay Rays. The organization who has significantly more at stake. If they trade away Archer, so will we. If they keep him, the long-term outlook is bright. So is the remainder of the 2017 season. Buy.

While Chris Archer toes the rubber against international competition, another pitcher will be abstaining from action: Sonny Gray. In defense of Gray, nearly this entire chapter has been dedicated to the horrors that could strike a pitcher who rushes his preparation before the regular season. Still, Gray's story *feels* unlike the rest. That's when I like to pay attention.

Believe it or not, the details behind Gray's absence from the

World Baseball Classic are not important. They actually get in the way. We don't want facts. We want perception. We want my subjective description of how this 'feels.' Not how it *is*.

If we were to rank the use of certain buzzwords that influence perception of a player, 'injury' would be near the top. So would 'fragile.' And 'offseason surgery.' But, nothing beats the use of the word 'insurance' when describing a player. Usually, someone is a makeshift 'insurance policy' for another – at which point we would be wise to avoid the player with the 'policy.' In the case of Sonny Gray, there are direct connections between his availability for the World Baseball Classic and actual insurance on his health.

Again, the details threaten to derail the message, and they have been left out intentionally. As a result of reading these words, you should be drifting *away* from the idea of owning Sonny Gray in your upcoming drafts. Certainly, he will pitch in Spring Training, but he will not take the ball in the World Baseball Classic. With-or-without specific details, these are negatives, right?

The biggest decline Sonny Gray will receive due to missing the World Baseball Classic will be solely confined to his draft stock. That's it. Failing to pitch against Italy does not actually mean Gray is hurt. It doesn't even mean he is an injury *risk*. But, he will be tagged as such.

Sonny Gray might not make 30 starts in 2017. He may not be effective. He may not deliver value worthy of being one of the first 100 players drafted in a fantasy league. But, if he were to fail miserably across-the-board, it has nothing to do with a preseason news story. And it would barely cost anything to take a chance on the upside.

Gray's value was already low entering 2017 because of his long injury history. Now, he is discounted further. He will bring such an inexpensive price tag that it would be irresponsible to let him go to another fantasy owner late in a draft.

When the time comes to compare Sonny Gray with another potential draftee, remember *why* he has fallen so far. Acknowledge the difference between preventative action – fear that a player *might* get hurt – and reaction – said player is *already* hurt. In fact, publicly mix the two. Voice your concerns. Tell the other fantasy owners about the dangers of owning a pitcher like Gray. Say, "Insurance."

Then, watch as a potential 'ace' falls into your lap.

4 THE ALBERS EFFECT

It had become a part of my daily routine. I would scour a few websites and flip through colored tabs on a Microsoft Excel sheet. Shortly thereafter, the statistics would be updated, followed by some sort of quality control check to prevent duplicate names or pitchers accidentally being credited for hitting statistics – with their own numbers, which were of no value to me.

A small sample size is often detrimental to statistical analysis, but it is also unavoidable, at times. Specifically, if we aim for long-term projections – season-long fantasy sports – we greatly value numbers that have accumulated over multiple years. But, when we are trying to calculate expected outputs on a daily basis, we need to consider players without a long history. Namely, recent call-ups or those who are finally getting a bigger share of playing time.

I couldn't afford to exclude anyone from the spreadsheet. If I decided to cut someone off my list later on, I would, but only at my own discretion. Casually, I set the limitations for the players' minimum plate appearances to zero. If a human being stepped into the batter's box for any recorded amount of time in 2016, I would know about it.

The players atop the leaderboards shuffled in-and-out as the

Mike Trouts of the world were eventually replaced by a pinch-hitter who delivered on his single attempt, only to then be supplanted by another. Nearly everyone I included was completely irrelevant to my efforts and interest.

Except Matt Albers.

A ten-year veteran now on his seventh team, Albers – a relief pitcher whose best counting contribution to a fantasy team is holds – would become a mainstay in my spreadsheet that served as both an entertaining anecdote and reminder as to the value of attaching a narrative to a number.

From the conclusion of the games on June 1st through the end of the season, Matt Albers would dominate the leaderboard for a few advanced statistics. His perfect batting average was impressive enough, but the new 'Jack-of-all-trades' produced so many unblemished numbers in such a short time that he would never relinquish his title. The number one contenders weren't close.

Albers' name sent a smile across my face every time I saw it ahead of the league's great hitters. Of course, I was staring at an anomaly – one that was not only impossible to repeat, but was utterly useless – but that's what made it beautiful. It was different. It was an exception. It was a constant variable.

I had been listening to the game since it started hours ago, mainly because it was my top pick for a low-scoring game in which both starting pitchers – Jacob deGrom and Miguel Gonzalez – were in my daily fantasy lineups. A 1-1 game in the 13th inning, my projection was correct, but I could no longer benefit from the outcome since both pitchers had long been removed. Now, I was simply enjoying some afternoon baseball on the radio.

Twelve innings had been completed. The Chicago White Sox were on their seventh pitcher of the day and, by virtue of playing in the Mets' National League ballpark, had no other option than to let their relief pitcher bat for himself. Lumbering into the batter's box with a body *slightly* larger than the average athlete – I faintly recall the radio announcers making a similar sarcastic comment – was

Albers. At the time, he carried a career batting average of .059.

Always a fan of chaos in sports, I leaned in and turned the radio up. I had just reached the parking lot where I needed to be, but had no intention of leaving the car before seeing this through. Matt Albers was batting in a tie game in extra innings! This could be something!

I cheered like a maniac. I'm not a White Sox fan. In that moment, I became one.

Albers sliced a fly ball into the gap in left-center field and powered his way to leadoff double. Genuine shock filled the airwaves. One wild pitch later, Albers was on third base. I'm squealing. Another few pitches. A long fly ball, a sacrifice fly, Albers races home and gives his team its second run in nearly thirteen innings of action.

I finally leave the car, beaming from ear-to-ear that I had just listened to absurdity in action, and I enter the building. I'm here to pick something up. So now I'm standing in line. With no headphones, I press the phone to my ear and listen as Matt Albers, the man who will, from this point on, be the most productive hitter according to a spreadsheet, takes the mound to finish the job. Sixty feet and six inches away from where he just delivered an improbable moment. And I wanted more.

I wasn't worried. An eerie calm settled in. This was baseball. A sport built on mystique. Only here could Matt Albers be transformed into a midseason hero. One that would barely be remembered.

He delivered. *Of course*, he did. Albers retired the first two batters he faced, walked the third, then induced a game-ending groundout.

The final line for Matt Albers from June 1, 2016:

1-1, 2B, R (game-winning run), 2 IP, W

Maybe not a 'perfect game,' but a perfect moment, for sure.

For the remainder of the year – after that battle, 120 days on which a regular season game was played - my spreadsheet was hijacked by Matt Albers. I would see his name, delete it, and smile.

Anyone who attempts to tackle the sport of baseball using statistical analysis has only the purest of intentions. Nobody wants to destroy the game or even filter it down to a single number – wins-above-replacement is hardly standardized throughout the industry. We just want to quantify it so that we can capture it and replicate its value to others.

It is difficult for my grandfather to truly, accurately explain to me how great Mickey Mantle was. He uses adjectives. Metaphors. Sometimes he will throw in statistics, but it isn't necessary. He gets the point across. But my biggest takeaway from the conversation is how great Mantle was compared to his peers.

How does he compare to today's players? Wouldn't my adjectives for Mike Trout be just as overstated as my grandfather's recollections of Mantle?

This is why we started down the road of assigning numbers to players, and why we never stopped. Generational gaps can be closed, so why not tighten up the present day debates, too?

We calculate and tweak until we are happy. We think we found something buried within the sport that we love, so we keep digging deeper.

Eventually, the names on our screens are nothing more than values in a log. Arbitrary Player X performed to the level of Y and, with some factor of error, can be projected to produce a value of Z for a fantasy team. Calculate. Tweak. Sort again.

And then there's Matt Albers.

Delete. You're in the way.

In the way of what? Of sorting other numbers? Of determining where other worthy players stand?

If so, we are completely devaluing Matt Albers. The man who, it could be argued, single-handedly won a baseball game, offensively *and* defensively. Of course, he had value! He was, in essence, the most valuable player to his team on one June afternoon in Queens.

By my innate urge to strike Albers from the system, I ran the risk of diminishing this moment. Statistically speaking, Albers provided nothing in the form of true value to me or my spreadsheet – it is actually the opposite, as the few seconds it took to delete him were, technically, wasted. But, what is the purpose of these numbers without the *sport* backing them up?

Clearly, the goal of the book is to find value wherever we can. But the use of such a mathematical term attempts to remove the emotion from the experience. We want to win. This is clear. But, we aren't trying to grow a portfolio through lifeless stock tickers. We are taking something we presumably love and finding ways to enhance it.

At one point, it shouldn't matter what Matt Albers or any other singular player contributes to my spreadsheet or our fantasy teams. We won't win every single day, so we best enjoy the ride, regardless. In the end, the game is bigger than all of us. Because of that, we love it.

Baseball fans love the anomalies. Those of us diehards live for the jaw-dropping moments, especially when they defy normalcy. A ball that ricochets off a base. A position player on the mound. A relief pitcher scoring the game-winning run.

Baseball might be the slowest, most repetitive sport in the world. That's what makes it beautiful. That's what makes it magical. Despite decades upon decades of watching nearly identical actions repeated constantly, we know that another outcome is *possible*. When it does, we tell the story. And the story makes the numbers memorable. Special. It turns a career .298 hitter with 536 home runs into *Mickey Mantle*. A 25-year old with five consecutive seasons of finishing in first or second place for MVP voting into *Mike Trout*.

We counter Albert Einstein's definition of insanity because we *love* the times when a repeated action provides a new result. Therefore, we *are* insane.

Really, we are just fans.

5 MINIMUM REASONABLE EXPECTATION

Fantasy sports may, indeed, be games of skill, but there is an undeniable level of 'luck' at play. Small or large, it is a non-zero factor. Unfortunately, our own efforts cannot influence said luck – 'freak accidents' are, by definition, irregular and, thus, unpredictable but we can somewhat decrease the factor by which luck impacts our fantasy team.

We will start with a few assumptions that must be accepted. With further research, they can probably be refuted. We don't want that. We want a conservative approach, and each of the axioms are built to achieve the goal of limiting 'dangerous' exposure.

Injuries *will* happen and, while we cannot pinpoint the aforementioned 'freak accident,' we can build in some cushion for those players who have had a history of missing time due to chronic ailments. If we can buy into a player that can only give us 100 games, then we would be pleasantly surprised if he delivered a full season. We will gladly welcome the additional contribution.

Many projection systems take into account an average of production over a specific set of time. Averages could be extremely misleading. If Player A hits 15 home runs for three consecutive seasons, and Player B had seasons of 5, 15, and 25 home runs, respectively, they both produce the same average of 15 home-runs-per-season. If we value consistency higher than upside, we would be targeting Player A. If we are in a position to target high risk-reward hitters, Player B is more appealing. Whatever the preferred plan-of-attack, don't take averages at face value.

Where a player bats in his respective lineup is critical to projecting output, both for daily fantasy games – as we will see in Chapter 9 – and season-long teams. For the sake of discussion, rumors about shifting the batting order hold little value until the player actually moves within the lineup. Don't buy in until you see it. Assume that said hitter will bat in a position no better than where he finished last season.

By now, it should be evident what we are trying to accomplish. We are creating a set of 'worst-case scenarios' that can be applied to our players and their respective projections.

With some governing rules established, we can condense them into a somewhat tangible variable. This yields the player's baseline. It is the minimum reasonable expectation. MRE, if you will. And, it has its own slogan that reads, "When in doubt, round down."

This is far from the first or last place where you will come across the desire to approximate a player's baseline – it is one of the most common practices in statistical analysis of fantasy sports – but it is worth highlighting when to use it and how much weight we assign to it and its components. As is the case with nearly everything in this world, proceeding on a case-by-case basis is preferred, where possible. If we can't, we will note the exceptions and where and why we adjusted as we did.

Returning to the axiom and example about averages, we can determine that, while Player A exhibited impressive consistency over a three-year period, Player B is actually the one we want to consider for our fantasy team. But, only if we use the *correct* number. That is, his minimum output of five home runs.

If we base this player's projections on the worst production he has had, we will pay a lower price and, thus, take a smaller risk.

Minimum Reasonable Expectation

Then again, if we are too conservative, we will almost certainly miss out on said player altogether, especially if he most recently delivered 25 home runs and is showing the makings of a potential 'breakout candidate.' How do we balance this?

We already accepted that risk is part of the game. Somewhere, we will have to take chances. Just not when the talent levels are thin.

Prior to the 2016 season, there was a debate within fantasy baseball circles as to whether or not Mike Trout or Bryce Harper deserved to be taken with the first overall pick. Quite frankly, this argument was silly. Trout had established himself as one of the best hitters in baseball over his previous four seasons, three of which featured no fewer than 157 games. Harper exploded in 2015 as the National League Most Valuable Player and deserved nothing but praise for his extraordinary performance. However, it was, indeed, *extra*ordinary.

Over Harper's previous three seasons – one of which was his rookie campaign, he played an average of 119 games-per-year. The worst indictment of this statistic is that his *rookie* year – 139 games played – was actually the season in which he played the most games – contrary to the typical career path, where a player would ease his way into the league. In fact, 139 games decreased to 118 games in 2013, then 100 games in 2014.

When given a nearly-full workload of 153 games, Harper delivered in a big way. In fact, if we focus on Harper's output-per-at-bat – a key metric – it was easy to project another stellar year, as long as he remained on the field.

Sometimes, it is that simple.

As long as Bryce Harper remained on the baseball field – i.e. not injured – he would deliver high returns. But what had led anybody to believe that he would repeat 153 games when he was already two full seasons removed from his previous high of 139?

Absolutely nothing.

The writing was on the wall that, indeed, he *could* repeat his performance, but it was more likely that he wouldn't be given the opportunity to do so. Harper ultimately played in 147 games – a surprisingly high number, given the history – but was a far cry from the 'best player in baseball.' His numbers took a dramatic dive in the categories of runs scored, runs batted in, hits, doubles, and, most noticeably, home runs and batting average. Not only did he miss some time, but he appeared to be playing through injuries that didn't quite force him out of the lineup and resulted in a catastrophically bad return on investment.

Despite his upside, taking Bryce Harper with one of the top few picks in 2016 was simply not worth the risk. Harper was not necessarily the only player to disappoint – Clayton Kershaw and Paul Goldschmidt come to mind – but he should have been the least surprising compared to his average draft position. And, if a fantasy owner actively decided to select Harper over Trout, he or she was certainly burned as Trout put together *another* MVP campaign.

The analogy between Players A and B concludes with the difference between consistency and upside relative to risk. In the first round – in the case of Trout and Harper, the first two picks of a draft – we want consistent excellence. We want Trout. In the later rounds, we want to pay for Player B's upside at his lowest price. We want Harper at a discount.

Thankfully, there are always an abundance of players whose minimum baseline is within reasonable expectations. Sprinkle in upside and we have our first set of 'sleepers.' Most are 'rebound candidates.' Here are a few for the 2017 season:

Jose Bautista – A consensus early-round pick for the last half-dozen years, Bautista's explosion into the upper echelon of fantasy hitters finally fizzled. It did not, however, completely diminish. The Blue Jays' slugger – who just had his streak of six consecutive years with an All-Star appearance snapped – saw virtually every one of his important statistics suffer in a 'walk year' in 2016, but he gets a mulligan in '17 with basically another one-year contract. With 2014-

2016 featuring home run totals of 35, 40, and 22, respectively, we can find immense room for growth if we pay the price for 22 home runs – a later round, since Bautista's stock has plummeted – and receive anything more by season's end.

Dallas Keuchel – The write-up on Jose Bautista should act as the template for the majority of this group, as evidenced by sliding seamlessly into a breakdown of Dallas Keuchel. His last three seasons' earned run averages are 2.93, 2.48, and 4.55. Granted, Keuchel doesn't have the same longevity in his resume as Bautista, but the Astros' 'ace' pitcher is only one season removed from winning the Cy Young award. Most importantly, Keuchel did not concede *every* category in his 'down' year, as he was still an excellent source of strikeouts-per-inning-pitched. With one statistic stabilized, the rest can follow.

Felix Hernandez – A third 'rebound candidate,' Felix Hernandez is arguably the most consistently *great* player of the aforementioned group. He has the long-term track record of success that dwarfs that of Keuchel, while also winning the developmental race to stardom – Bautista was a non-factor for the first six years of his career, while Hernandez continually blossomed as expected. The knock on the Mariners' 'ace' is that he has now delivered *two* consecutive underwhelming seasons, but it would be naïve to ignore his previous seven years, during which he finished in the top-four of Cy Young voting four times – winning once.

Miguel Sano – A 'sleeper' of a different sort, Miguel Sano's downward spiral does not stem from previous success that has failed to be repeated. It stems from simply missing expectations. Sano's calling card is power and, while he certainly has the ability to launch nearly any pitch over the fence, his 25 home runs in 2016 are easy to lose in the shuffle. What Sano does have in his favor is the pedigree of a once-top-prospect now entering his third season. It is extremely plausible that another offseason of work will benefit Sano drastically, and we would be barely risking more than a bench spot to secure his incredibly high ceiling.

Brian McCann – After playing in Yankee Stadium – a left-handed power hitter's dream venue – it seemed impossible for Brian McCann to land in an equally-desirable situation. Perhaps his new ballpark isn't as ideal as his old one, but Brian McCann shifting to the deep lineup of Houston is a fair tradeoff. At a position that remains relatively scarce – of course, after the top players – McCann will likely see an increase in opportunities to drive in runs, maintain his power output, and still reap the rewards of playing in the American League by serving as the team's designated hitter when he is not catching.

Anthony Rendon – The story of Anthony Rendon never changes. He holds incredible upside, but simply cannot stay on the field long enough to reach it. At least, not consistently. Thankfully, alternating years of full-length and shortened campaigns help further the perception that Rendon "never" stays healthy. It isn't true, and his 156 games in 2016 marked the second time in three years that he reached the 150-game barrier. Rendon does suffer slightly from losing his eligibility at second base, but otherwise is an overlooked asset in a deep lineup.

Rajai Davis – The speedster may have made it into the introduction of this book thanks to his power heroics in the World Series for the Cleveland Indians, but Rajai Davis now has a new home atop the Athletics' lineup. By virtue of shifting from the American League champions to an Oakland organization that has struggled in recent years, Davis is suddenly a forgotten talent. It would be wise to remember that he has stolen at least 34 bases in seven-of-his-last-eight seasons and can be acquired at an incredibly low price.

Michael Brantley – The opening to this chapter creates the ideal bookend for the finale where we can, again, assess a level of risk we are willing to take based on an expected price tag. Let's ask ourselves a pair of questions. If Michael Brantley plays a full season, can he produce early-round value? Absolutely. But, *will* he play a full season of Major League Baseball? According to his track record, it is unlikely. Attempting to project the amount of games Brantley plays might truly be riskier than drafting him altogether, but we can use our simple rule as a protective measure: round down. Whatever contributions we project from Brantley, we can conservatively slash them. We know how high his potential is, but reaching it would be nothing more than icing on an inexpensive – but good – cake.

6 MAXIMUM EXPOSURE

Of the four major sports, baseball is arguably the most fascinating in a fantasy context. Statistics are already revered, and there is an insatiable desire to turn each element of the game into a standalone number. The player pool is so massive that our self-derived numbers can be attached to basically anyone who might make an appearance in Major League Baseball – including prospects. By virtue of the ever-expanding glossary of advanced statistics, we could conceivably sort the entire league by any metric imaginable and produce a different result.

When we start expanding our list of players from dozens to hundreds to thousands, we can find some who share nearly identical numbers, yet also deviate wildly from the mean. With games played daily, we can even find role players to fill in at a moment's notice without a major decline in production over a short span of time.

Swapping out one player for another over the course of an entire season would *appear* to be more daunting than a simple one-time roster move – after all, no one wants to 'miss' during the draft – but, only if we are passing on an established, prime asset.

Certainly, it would be difficult to find Mike Trout's production in the later rounds and, if a 'sleeper' suddenly develops into the same superstar as Trout, he was already overlooked by so many fantasy owners – by virtue of being drafted so far after Trout – that we can't fault ourselves for doing the same. With the exception of the elites, there will almost always be a way to approximate one player's value with another. Usually, at a lower cost.

The previous chapter helped us identify players who could contribute to our fantasy roster without the risk of crippling it entirely. But, fielding a team constructed entirely of bargain purchases will likely result in a mediocre season. We need *some* explosiveness. Just not the type that will blow up our roster.

Until now, we have been looking at the 'buying' side of the drafting equation. We are accumulating assets that fit our cautious budget. But, smart purchasing also requires knowledge of the sale, as well. If we trust that we can replace practically any player we don't draft, the next question to ask is, "How can we pinpoint the players to avoid?"

The landscape of Major League Baseball is ever-changing, and it tends to get segmented into different 'eras.' We have all heard of the 'Dead Ball Era' and many people can still recall the onset of the 'Free Agency Era,' but we can all acknowledge that we are currently living in a transitional period out of the infamous 'Steroid Era.'

Some would argue that performance-enhancing drugs are not only still prevalent in the sport, but will *never* be completely eradicated. Perhaps. But a few key numbers indicate that we are undeniably moving out of the 'Steroid Era,' itself.

Home run totals and the average age of hitters are two of the metrics that saw a rapid increase to eye-popping levels. Not only were batters slugging home runs at a record rate, but hitters were generally enjoying longer careers than their predecessors. And when did this 'boom' occur?

20 of the 21 most productive power seasons – in terms of home-runs-per-game – were recorded from 1994 to 2016. The other season that slipped into the top-21 ranking was 1987 – which

was often rumored to be linked to steroid-use.

All nine seasons from 1998 to 2006 ranked in the top-13 for league-wide home run rates. Rates began declining as quickly as 2007 – albeit, in a scattered, non-linear fashion – and, by 2015, we were witnessing a league more closely related to an average season found in the 1990s. Granted, 2016 was one of the most power-laden years in history, but the overall pattern of home run rates from the past few decades forms a 'bell curve,' where we are clearly on the backend of the peak.

Unlike home run rates, hitters' ages have varied throughout the past century for far too many reasons to *directly* link performance-enhancing drugs as the undisputed source. Still, we can use baseball's predetermined eras as cutoff points and draw similar conclusions.

Confining the time period to the last 30 years, we find that the high points for the average age of a hitter in a given season fall directly in the middle of the power surge from 1998 to 2006. We may not have indisputable evidence with isolated variables, but we can certainly proceed with the broad understanding that diminished home run numbers and a gradual decline in players' ages are linked. Following the 'bell curve,' it appears as if Father Time is recouping some of his losses from the previous decade or two.

More than ever, we need to consider age when attempting to project home runs for an upcoming season. Younger players who are finally emerging into their physical prime can be given a slight boost, but the typical veteran needs to be approached with caution. Surely, *some* can hold out, but a player advancing in age is, indeed, heading toward a cliff.

Admittedly, we may suffer from an obvious danger when factoring age into a home run equation: simply weighing it too heavily. Thankfully, if we follow the aforementioned rule about 'rounding down,' then our biggest mistake would be an output that is too conservative.

Of course, we could miss a player whose drop-off point is still years away, but this is greatly preferred to being too aggressive and paying a high price for a slugger who can no longer replicate his power numbers. Even if said player explodes, the risk was simply too high to justify the reward. Assuming he follows a normal career trajectory, he will decline and hopefully sink someone else's fantasy team in the process.

While players have outperformed their ages on a yearly basis, we will begin our 'advanced age' cutoff at 32 years old. The range of an athlete in his 'prime' certainly varies across all sports, but we must accept that the likelihood of a downtrend grows with each year after a player's 30th birthday.

We won't wait for the writing to be on the wall. We will give the player a few years into his 30's – technically, two – and then begin cutting bait. The difference between a 31 and 32 year old may be minuscule, but we cannot cherry-pick who will survive and who will crumble. This is a league-wide shift that has coincided with the eventual exit from the 'Steroid Era,' and no player is exempt from the increased time-to-decay.

Somewhat intentionally, one of the last steps I took when updating my fantasy baseball spreadsheet for the 2017 season was to plug in the correct age for each player. The numbers adjusted and four 32-year-old hitters were immediately devalued simply by virtue of their ages: Justin Turner, Daniel Murphy, Matt Kemp, and Derek Norris. All four of these hitters saw their power projections slashed because of one number growing past a cutoff point. Fair? Probably not. But cautious, indeed.

By the time the season begins – assuming there is no major news story that requires an adjustment to the numbers – I will almost certainly have a lower projection than the rest of the industry for Justin Turner and Daniel Murphy. The former teammates combined for *52* home runs in 2016, yet my spreadsheet for 2017 originally capped them at 14 apiece.

If we step away from the numbers, we can easily make the argument for Turner and Murphy repeating last season's success.

Both players appear to be developing power later in their careers, largely thanks to regular playing time. But, the sample size remains small and, at 32 years old, Turner and Murphy are likely already running out of time.

Perhaps their torrid paces *can* continue. In fact, I am fairly confident that Turner and Murphy will hit more home runs than I have projected for them. But, I want to remain on the 'selling' side of a pair of 32-year-olds who had failed to hit more than 16 home runs in a season every year prior to 2016. I might be selling too high *too quickly*, but I refuse to buy at these levels.

Turner, Murphy, Kemp, and Norris – the latter two were mentioned, but not discussed – all suffered from age moving them into a category of potential 'busts.' Essentially, they are tagged as such because the general expectations are significantly higher than the value I anticipate receiving from their production. However, 'busts' are not defined by age. They are created by market prices.

Here are some potential 'bust' candidates among younger players:

Bryce Harper – I dedicated nearly an entire section to him in Chapter 5 when discussing the non-debate of 2016's fantasy draft, and it is clear that I am usually the 'low-man' on Bryce Harper. The numbers are always going to impress, but the injury concerns are too great to risk with a first-round pick. Indeed, his ceiling might be the highest in the game – he already won a Most Valuable Player award – but his floor is too shaky. Harper would need to fall considerably – most likely, into the second round after I already secured a stud – for me to be comfortable drafting him.

Trea Turner – It is hard to find someone who loves prospects and youth in baseball more than I, but I am generally cautious with the inexperienced player flying up draft boards. Perhaps Trea Turner will justify his price tag, but I can't help but fear that his value is artificially inflated by a whopping .342 batting average and 33 stolen bases in 73 games, last season. It is just too easy to double his numbers and project an MVP-candidate. Will I be outwardly avoiding Turner? No – in fact, my spreadsheet ranks him extremely high. But his small sample size is likely much better than what we will receive over a full season, and someone else will probably pay the price before I would.

Gary Sanchez – In almost the same situation as Trea Turner, Gary Sanchez had such a ridiculous stretch of baseball in the latter portion of 2016 that his stock has risen to unsustainable levels. If last season extended into the months of November and December, I could justify buying into Sanchez until his hot streak ends, but he has now had an entire offseason of expectations continually rising. In addition to simple regression working against him, Sanchez will see his numbers suffer by virtue of catching for a full season. If his games are limited, his counting statistics are equally capped. Otherwise, the workload behind the plate might drag down the production that is projected – by too many people – to be outstanding.

Francisco Lindor – There is no denying that the offensive statistics have been excellent – and balanced – in Francisco Lindor's first two years of Major League Baseball – .306 career batting average with 31 stolen bases and 27 home runs through 257 games – but we should not forget about his initial scouting reports. That is, Lindor was touted as a glove-first shortstop – and his defense has not disappointed, in the least – whose bat was a bit more questionable. It is plausible that he developed at precisely the right time – give Cleveland credit for an accurate promotion – but he could be hitting his ceiling at a suddenly deep offensive position. His floor is high and relatively stable, but projection systems might be too generous by continuing to increase his career trajectory at the plate.

Andrew Miller – It was nearly impossible to not be captivated by Andrew Miller's performance in October – and, really, every game since he was acquired by the Cleveland Indians. The southpaw redefined the term 'bullpen ace' – a phrase I have every intention of coining, assuming it has not already spread without my knowledge – by virtually shutting down an opponent simply by walking onto the field. Unfortunately, most traditional fantasy leagues require relief pitchers to accumulate saves in order to deliver value. Stealing a few wins does help – and Miller will be given opportunities to do so – but projecting wins for a relief pitcher is risky. In the end, Miller's upside remains as capped by his expected lack of save opportunities.

7 YOU ARE ON THE CLOCK

We prepared. Identified players who could be bought on the cheap and those who will surpass our price range. Calculated risk and avoided the 'noise.' Given control over every other team in the league, we know how *we* would draft. But, what about the other owners?

The beauty of the age in which we live is that nearly everything is accessible through the internet. Not only can we find *how* other fantasy owners are ranking their players – by a multitude of websites from which their own conclusions are likely drawn – but we can actually watch the trends in real-time by going through the process side-by-side with an approximation of our competition.

There should be absolutely nothing at stake when we enter a draft room for the first time in a given season. We are here to learn, observe, and get comfortable with the methods of other owners. We are here to 'mock' the process of a real fantasy draft.

Mock drafts are often discounted by the fantasy sports world due to the lack of serious commitment from all participants. But, as usual, we look for something to gain in all areas of our preparation, and nothing we will experience prior to the start of the regular season is completely irrelevant.

Every attempt we make to better our fantasy sports career has a purpose. We just need to identify it.

Indeed, the amount of pertinent information gleaned from a mock draft is largely dependent upon the participants. If you are lucky enough to land a half-dozen like-minded fans, you are ahead of the game. We will, of course, assume the worst-case scenario is unfolding.

In the event that retired athletes or obvious bench players start getting drafted in the first few rounds, you will get an early feel for how the next half hour will unfold. If so, start to adjust your takeaways accordingly, and look for the areas where we *can* find helpful observations.

Regardless of how the mock draft unfolds, the following tips will help extract value from an exercise many will dismiss:
- Accept that nothing from your mock draft will actually happen in your real draft. Assume the worst. If a player 'falls' to you in your mock draft, pretend it didn't happen. If you are already considering said player at said point in the draft, you know you would pounce if the opportunity actually presents itself. You don't need to practice such an action.
- Always round down. Similarly to Chapter 5 – Minimum Reasonable Expectation – try to fill your roster with a player *lower* in your pre-ranked tier than you can afford. During your real draft, competitive owners will be more aggressive and you will, eventually, get sniped. Prepare to survive the sniping. Don't let it cripple your system.
- Even if drafting with only a few people – many will be absent and resort to 'autodrafting' – you should immediately be able to pick out patterns and trends. Forget about 'runs' on closers or those who get stolen bases, as that is too driven by desperation in the moment – which won't exist in a mock draft – but, instead, focus on which positions or

types of players tend to get clustered together in the rankings. The drafting software will typically rank players either by average draft position or projected statistics. For our purposes, these are relatively interchangeable, as we will see a 'chicken-or-egg' cycle, where the statistics drive the draft position, which was pre-ranked to assume the statistics. Regardless of the source, bundles of positions and types of players will present themselves at certain periods of both mock and real drafts.

- Always experiment with different draft slots and relative positions. Take a pitcher – Clayton Kershaw – first overall. Take three pitchers in the first three rounds. Take no pitcher until the fifth round, and make it a closer. Take the best available players at any position and see if you can create a balanced roster. Tinker. Don't destroy the draft, but experiment with what works best.
- Aim to fill categories later that were ignored in the early stages of a draft. Continuing on the theme of 'experimentation,' force yourself to find power, speed, or any other specific fantasy category late in the draft. This will help determine the scarcity of such an asset, and force your hand when the stakes are raised. Remember the tiny feeling of panic that set in when you couldn't find a hitter who will deliver a high batting average late in your mock draft, and apply it to your future plans-of-attack.

2016 concluded as one of the most power-filled seasons in Major League Baseball history. 2017 may not necessarily continue this trend – in fact, it may prove that last season was an outlier – but initial drafts confirm that the market is now over-saturated with home run potential. As a result, the former crop of 'reliable power' has been discounted. These players do come with a risk – mainly from age and injury concerns – but their price tags are no longer too steep to absorb the hit taken if one fails.

Giancarlo Stanton is getting drafted in the third round. Jose Bautista – in another 'walk year' – is going outside of the top 100 players. Mark Trumbo – who *led* Major League Baseball in home runs by nearly a ten percent margin over the next hitter – can easily be selected in the sixth or seventh round of a 12-team draft.

In addition to the possibility of the aforementioned players – or equivalents – falling off-the-map quickly, the power-first mentality of these hitters often comes with the compromise of batting average – Trumbo led the trio with a .251 average in 2017. So be it. We will target hitters with a high average elsewhere. Such as the early rounds that used to house these big-name sluggers.

Starting a team with Jose Altuve and Max Scherzer or a trio of Clayton Kershaw, Madison Bumgarner, and J.D. Martinez might appear light offensively, but both setups lock in outstanding pitchers and largely productive hitters who will hit for a high batting average. Any shortage of power can easily be added later. In another round, the first group could blossom to Altuve, Scherzer, and Giancarlo Stanton, while the latter team could start with Kershaw, Bumgarner, Martinez, Carlos Gonzalez, and Chris Davis. Suddenly, Davis' .250 career batting average – .221 in 2017 – is offset by the previous selections.

Pitchers appear to be following a similar trend to power hitters – dispersing the talent throughout the entirety of a draft – but only after the first few tiers. The output of Clayton Kershaw, Max Scherzer, or Madison Bumgarner is not as easily replicated as the home run potential of a Manny Machado or Anthony Rizzo. Don't sweat the loss of a single slugger. Sweat the loss of a top ace.

For this reason, it is actually *imperative* to draft a top-flight pitcher in one of the first two rounds. We can even go as far as drafting two such arms in the first three rounds. The other selection – or one of the other two, if only targeting one pitcher so early – would ideally help with batting average, as we already established.

Specifically honing in on one player, I have advocated taking

Clayton Kershaw second overall for the past two seasons – behind only Mike Trout, although I would take Kershaw first overall in a keeper league. While my projections might slide the southpaw behind Mookie Betts and Nolan Arenado, he still remains extremely high on my list. Worthy of debate, yet again, for the first overall selection.

It isn't even Kershaw's ridiculous production that jumps off the page. It is his ridiculous production at such a *consistently high level* compared to other pitchers that separates him from the pack. Certainly, Madison Bumgarner *could* give you Kershaw's numbers. Arrieta, too. But Kershaw *will* give you Kershaw's numbers. Because he does. Every season.

Admittedly, Kershaw does carry some risk – for basically the first time in his career – due to his recent back injury. But, this will likely result in a slight bargain. He may not fall far enough to consider him a 'steal' – in fact, in the area I am suggesting we draft Kershaw, he would be a 'reach' – but his newly decreased value allows anyone with a top-seven pick to realistically formulate a gameplan that includes Kershaw on his or her roster.

Missing out on Kershaw in the first round will almost certainly lead to chasing a top pitcher in the next few rounds. Perhaps the aforementioned Bumgarner or Chris Sale can fill the void, but we are now three or four pitchers deep and competing with other fantasy owners to select the one we prefer.

Looking at the first few rounds, we could have conceivably landed a trio of Kershaw, Carlos Correa, and Edwin Encarnacion or something like Nolan Arenado, George Springer, and Corey Kluber. Either would be sufficient, but I prefer the top pitcher in the game to be paired with outstanding hitters. There are many.

One we dive into the pool of bats to target for our teams, we quickly discover how the shift toward power has also resulted in a move *away* from stolen bases. Coinciding with 2016's home run rate – second-highest in history – the average amount of stolen-base-attempts-per-game reached its lowest point since 1967. Not only did we see an abundance of power, but we are witnessing the creation of a new 'scarcity.' We used to confine this to positions, but it now must be transferred to category specializations.

The massive 'slugger' who will deliver fifty home runs may still carry a premium – only one player has done it in the past three seasons – but, even if he were to reach a high milestone, the gap between him and the average player has shrunk. Simply put, hitting forty or fifty home runs *was* impressive when fantasy leagues' waiver wires were littered with middle infielders who could barely scrape the outfield wall. Now, nearly every hitter has double-digit home run potential.

We can basically do a direct swap between the desire to secure power categories and true stolen base scarcity. Where we used to crave the multi-category output – home runs, runs batted in and, to a lesser extent, runs scored – that Chris Davis provided, Khris Davis in 2016 afforded the same opportunity at an insane discount. With the savings, we could have paid up for a stolen base specialist.

Entering 2017, we will place a large importance on securing a player who has displayed a willingness to run over the longterm. Thankfully, the trend of increasing power and decreasing speed appears stable enough that we should not be tricked into the league suddenly having an influx of base-stealing threats. In fact, while many of this year's top prospects have some level of speed that would allow them to attempt a stolen base, it is clear that power is their calling card.

If we internally inflate the price of a stolen base specialist, we will almost certainly overpay at the time of the draft. Excellent. While we love savings at every level, the key to the game remains buying low and selling high. In this case, we plan to buy high and sell much, much higher.

This chapter covered my methodology used during fantasy drafts – both real and mock and, with the obvious exceptions of specific categories, the content is not restricted to baseball – but there were direct observations about players that are worth sharing. Here are some takeaways and comments regarding drafting a fantasy baseball roster in 2017:

- My desire to draft Clayton Kershaw early has not waned, as evidenced by the amount of paragraphs I have devoted to him in this book. The stability he brings to a fantasy pitching staff is unparalleled. When in doubt, take Kershaw.
- Despite recommending Kershaw whenever possible, there is no need to aim for a second-tier starting pitcher early. There are solid options strewn throughout the majority of the draft, and waiting for the right pitcher at the right time – never 'reaching' – will be rewarded.
- Similarly to starting pitchers outside of the top group, trust that a legitimate home run hitter will fall into your lap. Bypass one for another. Don't worry.
- Giancarlo Stanton is currently going in the third round of most drafts. This *feels* wrong. In any draft where I already secured a pitcher – or two – and a solid batting average hitter, I will be taking Stanton with my next pick. Kershaw and Joey Votto would be an ideal combination to start a team that soon adds Stanton.
- Assuming he isn't selected in the first few rounds, Dee Gordon is going to be the 'steal' of every draft. No pun intended. Any projection system that uses last year's statistics – including mine, although I adjusted for Gordon – will be thrown off by the lack of games he played in 2016 – due to suspension. I plan on owning him in as many leagues as possible. I will overspend, if necessary.
- Kris Bryant and Nolan Arenado are both usually drafted early in the first rounds, but it appears as if the flexibility from Bryant's position eligibility might be the tipping point for most fantasy owners. Not me. In reality, Bryant will usually be played exclusively at third base – and not outfield – potentially negating his edge. Both my spreadsheet and I

rank Arenado higher, and I would rather not pay for an added position that may not get utilized.
- The high number of starting pitchers that we can stockpile in the later rounds increases the value of closers. In essence, there are 30 closers for 30 Major League teams – give-or-take a few 'closers-by-committee,' injury risks, and likely candidates who have yet to be named to the role. After these pitchers are drafted, speculation takes over. But, we will also be speculating on our starting pitcher 'sleepers,' and the number of targets can increase daily. Pay more for the finite commodity: closers.
- Paul Goldschmidt is still a top-five pick. His .297 batting average marked the low-point of his last four seasons, but it ranked fourth among first baseman with at least 100 plate appearances in 2016. Other hitters at his position may post better power numbers – even that can be challenged – but he is the rare example of a complete fantasy package at first base. He did swipe 32 bags, last season.
- Players like Masahiro Tanaka, Matt Harvey, Max Scherzer, and Josh Donaldson are all suffering from some level of decreased pricing due to 'injury concerns.' The circumstance of each player's individual condition varies from one to the next – in the case of Tanaka, it is the *threat* of an injury, while Donaldson and Scherzer entered camp not exactly 100 percent healthy – but fear is now reflected in each player's price. Do not be overly aggressive when targeting one from this group – or any player with similar characteristics – but, as long as the outlook doesn't worsen, take the calculated risk in a round later than otherwise expected.
- Kyle Schwarber is being drafted – and ranked – as a fantasy baseball catcher. Kyle Schwarber is currently *not* a fantasy baseball catcher. At least, he shouldn't be. When Schwarber's 2016 regular season was cut short with a knee

injury, he had not yet gained eligibility at the catcher position for 2017. Some websites have made an exception and allowed him to remain eligible as a catcher, which boosts his value dramatically – he is listed as a catcher in my rankings, as well. But, pay attention to your specific league's settings to avoid overpaying for Schwarber the outfielder.

8 PAINTING THE BIG PICTURE

Any full-season projection system would be incomplete without forecasting the final standings for all 30 Major League Baseball teams. A viable playoff picture is crafted by looking months ahead from foundations built years earlier. We won't always land on the right numbers, but we will aim to move the teams in the right direction based on additions and subtractions, as well as a history of over-performing or disappointing.

The obvious road to profit from these predictions comes in the form of the win totals for each franchise. In March, almost every fan believes his or her team has a realistic chance to surprise. As a result, numbers get inflated to the point where we can sell aggressively. Conversely, if we find an organization that is outwardly being disrespected by the baseball world, we can buy and scoff in a few months when we hear an analyst shocked by this 'sleeper' team. Act accordingly by comparing the calculated win totals in this chapter with the ever-changing market.

In addition to finding value in the standings, projecting each team's final record is necessary for accurate fantasy expectations. A closer on a team capable of winning 100 games automatically receives a slight boost in his potential for saves, while a relief pitcher on a bad team will be relatively capped. These numbers do not have a subjective impact on a pitcher's value. They are directly calculated in my spreadsheet. There is a valid – albeit, convoluted – connection.

During the process of establishing teams' records for an upcoming season, I adjust the expected total of runs scored and runs allowed for each squad. These numbers get factored into a Pythagorean win-loss formula, and they slide directly into a few calculations for fantasy players. Hitters see their projected run totals adjusted with their team's numbers, while pitchers' win totals move with the amount of run support their teams should provide.

Here are the final standings for the last two seasons, including 'Projected' records from a Pythagorean win-loss formula from each team's actual runs scored and allowed throughout the given season:

American League East Division	2016 Actual	2016 Proj.	2015 Actual	2015 Proj.
Boston Red Sox	93-69	98-64	78-84	81-81
Toronto Blue Jays	89-73	91-71	93-69	102-60
Baltimore Orioles	89-73	84-78	81-81	83-79
New York Yankees	84-78	79-83	87-75	88-74
Tampa Bay Rays	68-94	77-85	80-82	81-81

American League Central Division	2016 Actual	2016 Proj.	2015 Actual	2015 Proj.
Cleveland Indians	94-68	91-71	81-80	84-78
Detroit Tigers	86-76	84-78	74-87	70-92
Kansas City Royals	81-81	77-85	95-67	90-72
Chicago White Sox	78-84	78-84	76-86	72-90
Minnesota Twins	59-103	66-96	83-79	81-81

American League West Division	2016 Actual	2016 Proj.	2015 Actual	2015 Proj.
Texas Rangers	95-67	82-80	88-74	83-79
Seattle Mariners	86-76	87-75	76-86	74-88
Houston Astros	84-78	83-79	86-76	93-69
Los Angeles Angels	74-88	80-82	85-77	79-83
Oakland Athletics	69-93	70-92	68-94	77-85

Beginning with the American League, we can draw a few conclusions from previous years' statistics that can help when planning for 2017.

- Despite winning the division in 2015 and 2016, respectively, the Blue Jays and Red Sox technically 'under-delivered' when securing the American League East. Each of the winners for the Central and West divisions over the last two seasons beat their projected records. Toronto and Boston likely suffered from a more balanced set of competition, where the East featured four teams with at least 80 wins in both '15 and '16. The Central and West cannot make the same claim.
- Texas was the only American League team to win the division in both of the listed seasons. The Rangers also over-performed in both seasons, and did so at an unsustainable rate in 2016.
- The Angels led the American League in 2015 with six more wins than their projected Pythagorean record would have suggested. They promptly lost six more games than their projected output in 2016. Los Angeles experienced a major 'correction.'
- Nearly every team in the American League Central has been able to win a few more games than their run totals –for and against – would indicate. With that, it is no surprise that the last three American League pennant winners have hailed

from the Central. Except, of course, the Twins.
- Minnesota's numbers were so atrocious that it should have been the worst team in Major League Baseball with a 66-96 record. It *was* the worst team in Major League Baseball, but distanced itself from the pack tacking on another seven losses.

Using history of teams' performances against their Pythagorean record as a guide and adjusting for offseason moves, we can create a series of notes for 2017, followed by the actual projections for the American League.
- Not only have are the Rangers over-extended, but they should have been an average team in 2016. Prepare for regression.
- The Mariners have steadily risen, as expected. They were asked to improve by eleven games from their 2015 record, and delivered ten more wins. They also added Jean Segura and Jarrod Dyson to go with a lineup anchored by Robinson Cano and Nelson Cruz.
- The strengths of the Red Sox and Indians – respectively, offense and pitching – are so outstanding that neither team will lose its grip on the division in 2017. Both will, however, concede more wins than in 2016.
- Cleveland's biggest risk to falling from the top of the American League Central was the failure to repeat its offensive output from 2016. The addition of Edwin Encarnacion should put an end to such fears. The team's pitchers – and bullpen with Andrew Miller – are dominant enough to keep the 'runs allowed' portion of the Pythagorean win-loss formula on the low end.
- Kansas City has outperformed its expected win total by at least four games in each of the last two seasons. The franchise also has two American League pennants and a World Series Championship on its resume in the last three years. The Royals have proven to be more productive than their calculations, and they have even added a few bats to

help boost the offense.
- Tampa Bay, Chicago, Minnesota, Los Angeles, and Oakland made up the worst five teams in the American League in 2016, and little hope appears to be in store for 2017. Long-term, Minnesota and Chicago have the young talent to progress, while Oakland has the best chance of the group to surprise today. Regardless, a playoff berth for any of these five teams in 2017 remains unlikely.
- The Tigers and Orioles keep knocking on the metaphorical door atop the division, only to get locked out – granted, Baltimore did secure a Wild Card berth in 2016. Both teams appear to be in a similar position entering 2017, with a rotation featuring two pitchers who dominated, last year, followed by a handful of liabilities.
- In 2016, Edwin Encarnacion's bat in the middle of Toronto's lineup allowed the Blue Jays to slide Jose Bautista to the leadoff spot and still maintain power in the middle of the batting order. Toronto has no such benefit in 2017, and the roster appears to be poised for a full-scale regression, including the pitching staff.
- The Yankees have been consistently competitive under manager Joe Girardi, and it is unlikely that New York completely falls apart in 2017. With one of the best farm systems in the sport, the Yankees have the cavalry one phone call away to make a late-season push at a Wild Card berth. Think back to the Astros of 2015 and replace Carlos Correa with New York's Gleyber Torres or Clint Frazier.

Below are the predicted final standings for the American League in 2017:

American League East Division	2017 Prediction
Boston Red Sox	91-71
New York Yankees	86-76
Toronto Blue Jays	84-78
Baltimore Orioles	79-83
Tampa Bay Rays	73-89

American League Central Division	2017 Prediction
Cleveland Indians	89-73
Kansas City Royals	87-75
Detroit Tigers	82-80
Minnesota Twins	75-87
Chicago White Sox	72-90

American League West Division	2017 Prediction
Seattle Mariners	93-69
Houston Astros	83-79
Texas Rangers	80-82
Oakland Athletics	77-85
Los Angeles Angels	68-94

Of the five predicted playoff teams in the American League, the Red Sox and Indians – two repeat division champions – are the more conservative picks to reach the World Series, while the Mariners are the most appealing in terms of upside. Seattle also has a true 'ace' in Felix Hernandez who can help anchor a postseason rotation and turn the Mariners into an ideal 'value' buy in March.

Performing the same exercise with the National League, we will start with the final standings for the last two seasons:

National League East Division	2016 Actual	2016 Proj.	2015 Actual	2015 Proj.
Washington Nationals	95-67	97-65	83-79	89-73
New York Mets	87-75	87-75	90-72	89-73
Miami Marlins	79-82	78-84	71-91	74-88
Philadelphia Phillies	71-91	62-100	63-99	62-100
Atlanta Braves	68-93	68-94	67-95	61-101

National League Central Division	2016 Actual	2016 Proj.	2015 Actual	2015 Proj.
Chicago Cubs	103-58	108-54	97-65	90-72
St. Louis Cardinals	86-76	88-74	100-62	96-66
Pittsburgh Pirates	78-83	78-84	98-64	93-69
Milwaukee Brewers	73-89	74-88	68-94	72-90
Cincinnati Reds	68-94	68-94	64-98	69-93

National League West Division	2016 Actual	2016 Proj.	2015 Actual	2015 Proj.
Los Angeles Dodgers	91-71	90-72	92-70	89-73
San Francisco Giants	87-75	90-72	84-78	89-73
Colorado Rockies	75-87	80-82	68-94	71-91
Arizona Diamondbacks	69-93	69-93	79-83	82-80
San Diego Padres	68-94	72-90	74-88	72-90

From the tables above, we can formulate some notes and observations about the recent history of the National League.
 - The Chicago Cubs *should* have won 108 games in 2016. In addition to the eerie similarity between Chicago's Pythagorean win total and the number of years in the World Series drought that just ended, the projected win

total is outrageous. The Cubs had the best record in Major League Baseball by *eight* games, and still could have done better.
- The New York Mets have played remarkably close to their Pythagorean records over the last two seasons. One potential explanation for this consistency is the 'extreme' nature of New York's roster. The Mets have an outstanding pitching staff that has been one of the best in the league at limiting opponents' runs, but the offense has scored at a below-average rate over the past two years. In fact, New York's offense was only a hair below the average team in 2015, which likely explains the better record – compared to 2016.
- The Nationals were criticized for a rather mediocre season in 2015, and rightfully so. Their projected 89-73 record would have put them within one game of the Mets for the National League East title. Washington responded with 95 wins in 2016 but, again, missed its potential.
- All six teams that were projected to win no more than 75 games – two in each division – did, indeed, stay below the barrier, but none collapsed. The biggest drop from a potential sub-75-win franchise was San Diego at 68-94, four games worse than the numbers expected. Philadelphia outperformed its Pythagorean record by nine games, the biggest number in the National League.
- Colorado failed to meet its projected win total in each of the last two seasons. The Rockies will enter 2017 with a new manager.

Finally, we conclude with predictions and notes for the National League in 2017.
- One likely explanation for the Cubs failing to reach the lofty goal of 108 wins, last season, was the state of the National League Central. Chicago won the division by 17 games and, at one point, the Cubs had no reason to push the envelope.

- The same is true for 2017, as Chicago's outlook is just as bright and does not necessarily *require* more than 100 wins to secure another division title.
- The opening paragraphs of this chapter hinted at teams whose win totals might be artificially inflated. The Los Angeles Dodgers are the prime example of such a franchise. Led by the best pitcher in the sport – Clayton Kershaw – the Dodgers are undeniably talented. But, their four consecutive division titles overshadow a few other teams in the National League West. San Francisco's pitching depth rivals that of Los Angeles and, if we factor in the Minor League system, the Giants actually have the edge. The battle for the West will be tight, yet again, but San Francisco is the sneaky play to slide to the top.
- As stated in the first set of notes, Washington did underperform in back-to-back seasons. But, the Nationals were easily able to overcome this relative 'disappointment' by winning a whopping 95 games – the second-highest total in Major League Baseball. Top-to-bottom, Washington is one of the most complete teams, and the Nationals can withstand improved competition within the division.
- The Mets cannot continue to lean on a one-sided roster that is also susceptible to injury. Filling a team with top-notch pitching is not a problem, but the fragility of young arms always puts the depth at risk. 2016 highlighted this exact issue and, without the offense taking enough steps to offset the dangers of relying solely on pitching, New York falls out of the playoff picture.
- The Marlins, Phillies, and Braves may not *directly* compete for a playoff berth in 2017, but none of the three are 'pushovers.' That title belongs to San Diego, an organization destined to hand free wins to the rest of the National League West.
- Colorado enters 2017 as the ideal 'sleeper' team – although

the Rockies are not-so-quietly gaining steam in the sports prognostication community. The team *will* reap the rewards of sharing a division with San Diego, the offense is clearly explosive – especially in Colorado's home ballpark – and the Rockies' pitchers, if graded on a curve, are no longer a liability. Colorado's 75-87 campaign in 2016 was unacceptable given the team's statistics, and the transition to manager Bud Black might be all the Rockies need to reach their potential.

Below are the predicted final standings for the National League in 2017:

National League East Division	2017 Prediction
Washington Nationals	93-69
New York Mets	85-77
Atlanta Braves	77-85
Miami Marlins	72-90
Philadelphia Phillies	70-92

National League Central Division	2017 Prediction
Chicago Cubs	102-60
St. Louis Cardinals	85-77
Pittsburgh Pirates	83-79
Cincinnati Reds	74-88
Milwaukee Brewers	65-97

National League West Division	2017 Prediction
San Francisco Giants	90-72
Los Angeles Dodgers	89-73
Colorado Rockies	86-76
Arizona Diamondbacks	77-85
San Diego Padres	63-99

Predictions for the National League yield only one new club in the playoff picture: Colorado. The Cubs and Dodgers are the obvious, 'safer' picks to reach the postseason – even though I have the Giants listed as the division winner – while Washington and San Francisco have the pitching to sustain a deep playoff run.

9 WIN THE DAILY FANTASY SPRINTS

Perhaps more than any other sport, baseball is particularly susceptible to randomness – ironically, in a book about 'accurately projecting baseball,' this harsh reality must be acknowledged. But, as unique as each instance of a round ball off a cylindrical bat is, the comparatively large sample size of a 162 game season does tend to produce consistency. At least, a high enough level of repeatable results to justify creating and trusting a projection system.

Conversely, boiling a full season's statistics down to a single plate appearance invites the opportunity to failure. The good news is that baseball is *the* sport built on failure, where limiting its exposure produces success.

Now that the daily fantasy sports industry has taken a foothold in the lives of countless sports fans, an ever-growing list of strategies and theories has emerged. In essence, each one is correct. They all can and will produce winning lineups. Of course, individual styles of play will result in different correlations between methodology and production, but experimentation is necessary.

The goal is to accept the viability of multiple options and be ready and willing to change from one to the next. Always remember, we aren't playing against a hard number. We are being ranked play-by-play against other fantasy owners, all of whom will employ their own malleable system.

At the end of the day, there is only one statistic that matters in the daily fantasy world: points. Certainly, *how* we accumulate enough points to win will be our next focus, but we cannot proceed without this understanding. Points are the only metric by which a roster is judged, and everything else is ancillary noise.

For the moment, forget about ownership percentages. Forget about salary caps. Forget the ratio between points and cost. Get points. Get more points than the other fantasy players. Points. Points. Points.

Now, we can work on how to accomplish this.

A first glance at the scoring system for daily fantasy baseball will almost certainly produce one of the easiest assumptions. I was guilty of it, too. That is, that the home run is the most valuable asset to obtain.

Home runs *are* the single-most impactful event to a fantasy lineup's score – positive or negative. And, since they are not completely impossible to predict, we can even create fairly accurate projection systems. We can. We do. But we also invite a huge opportunity to have our mindset shifted by an inflated perception of one of our factors.

Immediately returning to the introduction of this chapter, I want to highlight, again, the fact that points should be the only variable driving our initial decision-making process. But, we see the value in one swing of the bat, and we tend to chase it. More than we should.

The simple reality is that home run hitters – by virtue of their *potential* to deliver such a high point total in a singular moment – often carry a higher price tag. And, with even the best home run hitters delivering at a rate worse than one-home-run-for-every-three-games – think of someone slugging 50 home runs over a full 162 games; his rate is 3.24 games-per-home-run – we could easily have paid a premium for a hitter at the wrong time.

If all points are created equal, why not try to find the same potential as a home run hitter – after all, practically any batter in the game *can* put the ball over the fence – while also mitigating risk and saving salary?

One of the most commonly used strategies in daily fantasy baseball – really, most daily fantasy sports – is the 'stacking.' Essentially, fantasy owners would find a *team* in a good position and use as many players from said team's roster as possible. The theory is simple: if the team performs as expected, there will be plenty of points to go around.

It's true. 'Stacking' works. But, it works for everyone who employs it properly. The key, therefore, is finding the *right* way to 'stack' a team.

On-base percentage is quickly gaining popularity as arguably a better gauge of a hitter's production than batting average. I will neither advocate nor denounce either side of the debate but, instead, draw conclusions from both.

The majority of season-long fantasy leagues use batting average as the sole ratio statistic for a batter, and we can certainly project *how* a hitter should perform over a full season by using this metric. But, the dependence on batting average puts us in a dangerous territory if we try to use it for daily fantasy purposes.

The absolute best hitters in the sport – according to batting average – hit safely roughly one time for every three recorded at-bats. Unfortunately, 'recorded at-bats' do not include every one of a player's plate appearance for a given day. In fact, if a batter walks three times, advances a runner to third base on a groundout, and lines out to the shortstop, he is saddled with an 0-for-2 day. Alone, his .000 batting average for the game is far from telling the whole story.

Again, the numbers are not completely useless. If said hitter were to have a stretch of three or four games with similar outcomes, his 0-for-10 streak would present outstanding buying opportunities if he is currently trending below his baseline. This same player would have already been delivering fantasy value in daily formats, however, and this is where we can target our sneakier plays.

The strongest case in defense of unilaterally using on-base percentage lies in the root of what the number actually tracks. Borrowing the message from Michael Lewis' outstanding and insightful book, *Moneyball* – and other places in the sabermetric community – on-base percentage is essentially the rate in which a batter does not make an out. That's it.

In its simplest form, on-base percentage tracks how many times a batter approaches the plate and does anything in his power to reach base. There are, of course, exceptions in its more complex form, but we actually do not need to consider them. In fact, we can even approach on-base percentage conservatively and arrive at the same point.

A player's likelihood to 'not make an out' has so many positive repercussions on his team that we can essentially pick-and-choose how we want to apply it. In addition to the obvious fantasy points we would gain simply for the walks a batter would accumulate, it creates an opportunity for the same player to also steal a base or score a run. Most importantly, it moves the lineup one step closer to the player gaining another opportunity at the plate.

Somewhere in between these at-bats, other hitters are gaining the same benefits. Most likely, our on-base machine's ability to avoid making an out also resulted in advancing a baserunner – or actually driving him in. And, again, the lineup will continue moving. A batting order is cyclical, and preventing outs is often what leads to the belief that 'hitting is contagious.'

Runners on base – in most situations – force pitchers to deliver from the 'stretch' instead of the 'windup.' Of course, with some exceptions, the vast majority of pitchers prefer the full windup. Getting people on base takes a pitcher out of his comfort zone and, potentially, the game earlier than he would like.

Clearly, the bonuses gained by a high on-base percentage hitter are powerful enough that they should always remain on our radar. Specifically, Joey Votto and Miguel Cabrera carry such an incredible batting average to go with a high on-base percentage that we can always pencil them into our lineups. But this information is neither groundbreaking nor valuable, since it is common knowledge, at this point.

Our hidden gems are found buried within most of the benefits that I previously listed, mainly the ones that aren't directly assigned fantasy points. That is, advancing baserunners and moving the lineup around quickly. If Joey Votto and Miguel Cabrera are preventing outs in roughly two-out-of-every-five plate appearances, they are also likely advancing the lineup or a baserunner in the process.

We want these baserunners on our team.

We want the potential run that is driven in by Votto or Cabrera. We want the extra plate appearance. We want a batter who can 'catch' the contagious bug of hitting. And, we want these players at a discount.

Thankfully, the latter concern is almost always alleviated. Votto and Cabrera – and most consistently high on-base percentage hitters with general power – will usually cost more than their teammates.

It is always imperative to pay attention to the batting order as soon as it is finalized and released, but the necessity is enhanced when we are actively seeking players whose value depends on others. And the players we are targeting gain *another* boost by virtue of batting directly in front of Votto, Cabrera, or another slugger by gaining 'protection.'

Simply put, the threat of a better bat looming in the on-deck circle often forces pitchers to 'attack' the perceived 'weaker' option. This typically leads to better opportunities for the hitter in front of a superstar. He now becomes a fundamental piece for our lineup. Of course, he must also perform in order to actually contribute to our cause, but he is, at least, placed in a position to succeed.

As we have covered extensively throughout this book, baseball is a sport built on percentages and calculated risks. Like a Hall of Fame hitter, failure is unavoidable, at times.

We succeed by uncovering a foundation upon which a new strategy can be built. By considering factors that cannot be quantified. By winning the marathon comprised of small sprints on each passing day.

10 SHIFTING THE PARADIGM

If there are two areas in life I am quickest to dismiss, it is 'conventional wisdom' and the words of athletes. Whenever these are combined, I am compelled to run in the opposite direction, lest my ears be sullied with falsely accepted beliefs.

Hearing that a professional baseball player cannot hit a ball to the opposite field "because his swing doesn't allow it" or "it would mess with his psyche" or any other excuse spouted from the sports world regarding this asinine argument is infuriating. It is lazy. It aims to cover up a hole in a batter's game and it gives an excuse for a well-paid athlete to *not* have to adjust to the demands of his occupation. Instead, he will complain loud enough that fans and observers might actually take pity on him. Maybe they will go as far as dismissing this new movement instead of the player, himself.

The movement is, of course, the infield shift.

The statistics are obvious, and hardly worth reiterating. Defenses are positioning more infielders on the first base side of the field in an attempt to steal outs specifically from left-handed batters who *just can't help* but pull the ball toward right field. This gameplan is calculated and is beginning to deliver at such a high rate that it isn't going to leave. That won't stop its detractors from trying. Instead, complaints are growing louder that the shift should be banned.

Not so fast.

The infield shift is evolving. Developing into a seasoned veteran. Almost like a savvy pitcher without a *naturally* great pickoff move who can still catch a baserunner napping. But, only after said pitcher observes a tendency that can be exploited.

Tendencies are, after all, what drove opposing managers to slide infielders out of position in an attempt to turn a former base hit into an out. History would tell us that dead pull hitters – especially left-handed batters – could conceivably hit at least one-out-of-every-two balls in play to the right side of second base. Better than 50 percent odds for a sport based on predicting outcomes via positioning was simply too good to ignore. So no one ignored it. Not anymore.

Managers, pitchers, and defenses are openly challenging batters to hit the ball to the opposite field, yet it still happens so rarely that it fails to force teams to deviate from their plans. Again, we hear the excuses. I won't buy them. And I doubt many will. But, so far, enough of the actual players have accepted their fate that it might ultimately be too late to save them.

This is where the value comes in.

Somewhere in some minor league system or college program, an intelligent left-handed hitter – or his intelligent support staff – is watching the trends within the sport of baseball. Said hitter may not possess the raw power to vault him into Major League Baseball, but he might have just been handed a workaround option.

This hitter will forgo his desire to trot around the bases via the long ball and, instead, work tirelessly on the ability to hit a line drive to all fields. Had he broken into the league a half-decade earlier, expectations of power might have steered him in a different direction. But, now, seeing that he won't challenge any home run records, what does he have to lose by crafting a different skill?

A skill that would exploit an over-aggressive managerial

gameplan.

Said hitter's tendency to scatter base hits would undoubtedly force opponents to resort back to a standard defensive alignment. When that happens, he will, of course, lose his edge. But, not only will he regain a level playing field, he will already have mastered the art of hitting line drives for a high batting average. Major League Baseball teams will not pass on such a talent. Neither will we when construction our fantasy rosters.

Chapter 7 – You are on the Clock – included observations from drafts that highlight the need for owning some hitters who will help carry batting average. But, beyond the obvious players who now reside in the first few rounds of the draft, we will need to find batters who are already creating the movement we want. Left-handed hitters who will willingly hit the ball to the opposite field. So, I set out on this journey and returned pleased with my discoveries.

I deliberately chose to sort players in lieu of using their actual statistics in an effort to compare *intentions* instead of outcome. Without any true baselines for gauging spray charts – e.g. 100 works as a key number for runs batted in, while .300 is an impressive milestone for a hitter – I only wanted to know which players hit the ball to the opposite field more often and more successfully than the rest. Not to the level of an All-Star or defined replacement player, but compared to his peers.

The list I generated featured exciting similarities throughout distinct groups:

Joe Mauer and Joey Votto – A pair of future Hall-of-Famers – at least, I have argued vehemently in their favor in the past – might be on the downside of their careers, but have undoubtedly helped extend their production by using the entire field. Mauer and Votto have enjoyed a decade of success at the plate and should each serve as a shining example for a left-handed batter's approach to hitting.

Adam Eaton, Odubel Herrera, and Travis Jankowski – What does this trio have in common? Basically, everything. They don't necessarily hit for power – especially by 2016's raised standards – they can all swipe a bag, and each has turned an increase of playing time into a boost in batting average. Eaton and Herrera have a combined five seasons of a .284 batting average or higher, while Jankowski more than tripled his plate appearances from his rookie season and boosted his average 34 points in the process. Jankowski is a clear cut below Eaton and Herrera, but all three are willing to take advantage of a defensive alignment wherever possible.

Josh Bell, Brandon Nimmo, and David Dahl – My favorite group. Three young hitters, former solid prospects in their own right, and all of whom made their Major League debuts in 2016. The trio is poised to take down the infield shift in the near future – at least, when each one individually steps into the batter's box. The sample sizes are obviously small, but all three rookie campaigns – and the comparative rate with which they hit the ball to the opposite field – were encouraging based on the message behind this chapter. If we want to ride the wave *before* it crests, buying Bell – a switch-hitter – Nimmo, or Dahl is strongly advised.

11 BEGINNING'S END

Years from now, one wave of baseball players will be pulled out to sea, while another one violently races toward the shore. Left-handed batters with an 'opposite field approach' will not be the only ones to step into the limelight. There are, of course, dozens upon dozens of prospects to consider from all corners of the sport.

After playing in so many 'redraft' leagues – fantasy leagues in which a new team is drafted every year – it was only natural for me to sprinkle in a few 'keeper' leagues. Once I started, there was no going back. The player pool suddenly expanded to all levels of minor league systems, and I was feverishly researching players who had just attended their senior proms in hopes that one would help my fantasy team years down the road. I loved every minute of it.

Those of us who put our predictions and methodology behind our decisions on-the-line often feel a certain level of commitment to seeing our ideas through to completion. The ideas that avoid the cutting room floor are not just one-off thoughts that randomly appeared. They are dissected and calculated, and each one becomes our 'brainchild.'

I felt the same level of attachment to the players I have targeted in deep keeper leagues over the years. I drafted or acquired them. I committed resources – roster spaces – to them. I want them to succeed, and I want to see it happen, myself.

Unfortunately, so does everyone else. Before we know it, every 'top prospect' is owned, and the bench spots that used to house actual bench players – from Major League teams – now hold reserves for the prospects that might not ever develop. The pool is constantly growing thinner.

Naturally, the only move we can make is to look harder. To dig deeper. As usual, to see what others don't.

Each year, a new crop of prospects will emerge that needs to be analyzed and sorted. Unlike typical fantasy drafts – where the average position a particular payer has been selected by thousands of other owners is known to all – ranking players without comparable standards allows subjectivity to drive decisions. We should welcome this. It is the best way to find imbalances and tip the scales in our favor.

In the end, we should always be looking to cast aside the values that others have placed on our potential assets. Our competitors are only responsible to set the market price. But, we know what it is truly worth.

We find the edge. We act. We profit.

Many of the deep keeper leagues do not allow players to be drafted to a fantasy team until they are officially part of a Major League Baseball organization or one of its minor league affiliates. The following is a list of long-term prospects who became eligible for most fantasy leagues as of 2016's First-Year Player Draft and international signing period, ranked in order of draft preference:

Nick Senzel – Nick Senzel may have been the second overall selection in the 2016 draft, but he tops my list for first-year eligible fantasy players. At any point during a deep fantasy draft, I am seeking existing development over future plans – regardless of a player's position. For that reason, I will almost always lean on the college player compared to one out of high school. Senzel was widely considered one of the best bats in college – if not, *the* best bat – and his current position makes him a rarity among the top prospects in the sport. Outfielders are being produced at such a high rate – Moniak, for one – that their collective value will suffer, as a result. A third baseman with a high floor in a bad team's minor league system, Nick Senzel won't cost a fantasy owner years of waiting and should be ready to produce at a now premier position as soon as he steps on the field.

Braxton Garrett – Like hitters, I am always inclined to give the edge to college pitchers, but mainly because their road to a Major League club is much shorter than that of an arm fresh out of high school. If advancement through the minor league system appears to be a non-factor, however, then we could potentially be poised to secure a decade-long investment on the mound. Miami's Braxton Garrett fits the mold perfectly, and the southpaw – organizations tend to pour extra resources in developing left-handed pitchers - was in the conversation of 'best pitchers in the 2016' draft, despite being the fourth selected – seventh player overall.

Jason Groome – Now with Chris Sale and David Price in the Major League rotation, why wouldn't the Boston Red Sox keep stockpiling talented southpaws? Jason Groome was rumored to be *the* top pick in the 2016 draft class, but fell eleven slots before being selected with the twelfth overall pick. Thankfully for Groome's development, him slipping in the first round appears to be less about his on-field stature and more about personality. Of course, this could hamper his potential, but he is no more risky than the majority of high school pitchers, while possibly carrying the biggest reward.

Riley Pint – While I hate to take the 'obvious' road anywhere, for Riley Pint – a right-handed pitcher – Colorado was certainly a less-than-ideal landing spot. Talent-wise, Pint is off-the-charts, but he has years to go before he displaying it in a Major League ballpark. Unfortunately, unless he is traded, said ballpark will be the Rockies' hitter haven, and Pint's career numbers could certainly suffer. Then again, there are so many moving parts that it is not worth worrying about the venue for Pint's eventual masterpieces, right now. In fact, placing too much weight on a prospect's *current* situation is a surefire way to miss everything else he offers.

Mickey Moniak – After already admitting that I largely prefer to wait on high school hitters, Mickey Moniak is the one exception I would make early in a first-year fantasy draft – the last high school hitter I selected with a top-six pick was Clint Frazier. Moniak earned enough praise from Philadelphia's scouting department to warrant being selected first overall in 2016, and he appears to be such a complete hitter that few holes will prevent him from getting to the big leagues – if anything, delaying his service time in Philadelphia might be his biggest obstacle. Still a teenager, Moniak's power should blossom, as well.

Kyle Lewis – What ended up as a mid-first-round-pick in 2016 could have arguably developed into the most impactful player of the class in the shortest time. That is, until tragedy struck. Kyle Lewis is a college hitter with power potential in a farm system for a Major League club currently ready to compete. The stars were ready to align for Lewis until fate turned against him, knocking him out of the game for a year with a knee injury. The current expectation is that he will return to action sometime in the summer of 2017 and should begin tearing the cover off the ball immediately.

Kevin Maitan – Drafting Kevin Maitan in a keeper league is not for the impatient. The switch-hitting shortstop is only 16 years old, but is largely considered one of the best international signings in recent history. He already has exceptional power for his age and position, and it is nearly impossible to find a scout who could identify a flaw in his offensive game. Maitan is an elite prospect who has drawn comparisons to Miguel Cabrera – lofty expectations, for sure – and is everything we would want in a prospect if we are willing to wait.

A.J. Puk – A.J. Puk was another highly-coveted arm in the

2016 draft who seemingly could have been selected anywhere in the first dozen picks. Coming from the University of Florida, Puk has as good a foundation as any, but his stock did slip as he approached the end of his college career. In addition, there are whispers that Puk might be better suited for a bullpen role, which would severely cripple his long-term fantasy appeal. The good news is that Puk's road to Major League Baseball is relatively unblocked, as he will celebrate his 22nd birthday in April and was drafted by an organization that is not exactly bursting with consistent long-term rotation options.

Delvin Perez – Like the aforementioned Jason Groome, Delvin Perez fell in the 2016 draft due to off-the-field issues – in the case of Perez, it was related to performance-enhancing drugs. Removing the consequences of Perez's actions – any suspension would likely not impact his eventual Major League debut – the shortstop was one of the most talented players in the draft. St. Louis made a prototypical 'value buy' when selecting Perez at a relatively low cost. We may not be afforded the same luxury, but the shortstop position has become so deep in prospect pools that missing Perez wouldn't be the end of the world. If he is available, however, he presents the ideal 'buy-and-hold' candidate in an organization that would once-again welcome the idea of finding stability in the middle of the infield.

Eric Lauer – One of my favorite personal picks of the last few first-year player drafts was Aaron Nola, not because of his potential, but the rate in which he was expected to – and did – make his Major League debut. Especially when it comes to pitchers, we want actual Major League production in these deeper leagues. There is always a tendency to stockpile prospects and watch their value rise, but they are otherwise irrelevant to our team's standings until they get the call to the top level of the organization. By those standards, San Diego's Eric Lauer might present the quickest return-on-investment for pitchers from 2016's draft. The left-handed pitcher will turn 22 in June, has established himself as a starter, and is basically unblocked by the current starting rotation. He may not have the star potential of a few other arms in the draft, but he will likely have the opportunity to prove himself before most.

APPENDIX I – TOP 500 PLAYER PROJECTIONS

Season-long projections are, by definition, suited to provide an expectation for a player over the course of 162 games. This full season may serve as the perfect sample size – especially since it spans the hotter months of the summer, bookended by colder months – but it also covers so much time that changes are inherent. Simply put, the lineup in April will almost certainly vary dramatically from the one in September – or even, August, before the rosters expand.

Projected playing time is not linear. It compounds on itself. It is flexible and determined largely by on-field performance – there are exceptions driven by salary and contract language. If a player gets off to a hot start in April, he may lengthen his metaphorical leash and get more at-bats in May than he was expected to see, all season. Suddenly, his numbers are inflated, while also decreasing the potential for the player behind him on the depth chart. Conversely, struggling in the first few weeks could cripple the ability to recover, even if the player was simply in the middle of a 'cold stretch.'

We cannot attempt to plot out any singular player's season

trajectory unless there is a clear off-the-field factor behind it – such as the Cubs and Astros delaying the eventual promotions for Kris Bryant and George Springer, respectively, during their rookie campaigns. Instead, we must consider numbers spread across the full season and *incorrectly* assume that they can be applied to any given month.

Walking into a trap is slightly less dangerous when we can acknowledge its presence. As long as we are conservative in our approach, we should take less damage than the unsuspecting victim. In this case, we can 'round down' the number of projected games played or plate appearances to offer us some protection.

Each hitter is given a projection for games played, runs, runs batted in, home runs, stolen bases, and batting average. The 'counting statistics' – of the five listed categories, everything except batting average – are all driven by the projected amount of games played.

Once we acknowledge the avenue for error, we can be open to the idea of adjusting the number of games in which we expect a batter to participate as the season progresses or news emerges. Injuries and official lineup decisions take precedence. And, since estimating the number of games played – and, by extension, plate appearances – is the only piece of the formula with some level of subjective opinion included, it is the area most likely to be 'missed' by the majority of the industry.

I have included secondary tables that replace 'counting statistics' with per-game and per-inning projections for hitters and pitchers, respectively. The differences between the tables are noteworthy, and they illustrate the impact of playing time on potential output.

Purchasing this book also grants limited-time access to many of the features of Sporfolio – see the Additional Access chapter in Appendix II for details – including the updated spreadsheets for the tables in this chapter. Even if you have little interest in any other content provided by Sporfolio, it is advised to download the baseline numbers and input them into your own spreadsheet.

Top 500 Player Projections

Here are the 2017 fantasy baseball statistical projections for the top 500 players – the 'Ovr' column refers to the player's overall ranking, including all positions – starting with hitters:

Hitter	**Ovr**	**G**	**R**	**RBI**	**HR**	**SB**	**BA**
Mike Trout	1	159	101	95	35	24	.313
Mookie Betts	2	158	103	94	34	21	.307
Nolan Arenado	3	158	108	116	38	4	.298
P. Goldschmidt	5	158	101	102	28	20	.317
Kris Bryant	6	158	112	91	42	5	.302
J. Donaldson	7	158	107	96	44	5	.293
Starling Marte	8	150	86	86	21	35	.301
A.J. Pollock	9	130	103	61	18	44	.287
C. Blackmon	10	140	108	74	21	21	.306
Jose Altuve	11	159	96	76	16	32	.316
Bryce Harper	12	140	86	88	33	17	.293
Nelson Cruz	13	135	86	99	38	2	.305
Miguel Cabrera	15	150	90	101	28	0	.333
Anthony Rizzo	16	155	97	101	32	7	.290
J.D. Martinez	17	140	89	89	31	4	.316
F. Lindor	18	158	94	87	24	17	.306
Brian Dozier	19	157	103	75	50	12	.255
Buster Posey	20	140	83	92	22	5	.312
Trea Turner	21	145	102	79	13	31	.302
Ian Kinsler	22	155	104	77	32	14	.292
M. Machado	23	160	94	86	32	6	.293
Jose Bautista	24	150	94	100	39	4	.261
Y. Cespedes	25	150	89	97	33	3	.290
C. Gonzalez	29	145	92	108	30	4	.277

Diamond Dividends: Creative Strategies to Profit Through Fantasy Baseball

Hitter	Ovr	G	R	RBI	HR	SB	BA
Jonathan Villar	30	130	83	57	16	46	.281
Kyle Schwarber	32	140	105	80	21	0	.302
G. Stanton	33	135	78	101	35	0	.297
F. Freeman	35	155	92	89	25	6	.311
Gary Sanchez	36	130	86	98	24	3	.282
Chris Davis	37	155	92	101	39	1	.268
Jose Abreu	38	155	81	100	31	2	.302
Khris Davis	39	150	84	95	38	3	.272
Dee Gordon	42	150	95	49	3	53	.287
Joey Votto	43	157	92	83	25	7	.314
Todd Frazier	44	155	80	84	41	8	.261
G. Springer	45	145	96	75	29	14	.272
Justin Upton	46	150	81	92	29	10	.281
A. McCutchen	47	150	89	92	23	9	.292
Odubel Herrera	48	160	85	69	19	23	.292
Trevor Story	52	150	86	93	32	8	.279
Matt Kemp	53	155	84	102	27	2	.286
Robinson Cano	54	159	94	94	24	3	.307
Ryan Braun	57	130	81	86	25	10	.294
E. Encarnacion	58	150	91	111	26	3	.276
Jean Segura	59	150	90	66	18	31	.276
Mark Trumbo	60	145	77	91	37	2	.276
Corey Seager	61	158	99	73	26	2	.315
Albert Pujols	63	150	78	98	39	3	.264
Kyle Seager	64	155	82	91	30	3	.279
Adam Jones	65	155	93	83	30	4	.274
X. Bogaerts	66	158	97	87	21	8	.293
Carlos Correa	67	155	84	97	23	12	.281
Adrian Beltre	68	135	85	88	20	3	.309

Top 500 Player Projections

Hitter	Ovr	G	R	RBI	HR	SB	BA
Christian Yelich	70	155	86	79	14	13	.305
Daniel Murphy	76	155	92	93	13	7	.316
Carlos Santana	78	158	90	81	36	9	.249
Justin Turner	79	145	86	91	14	4	.310
A. Gonzalez	80	156	79	103	28	2	.280
Kole Calhoun	82	158	91	76	31	4	.271
DJ LeMahieu	83	150	106	75	12	8	.317
Rajai Davis	84	135	89	60	9	37	.259
Adam Eaton	85	155	100	60	18	11	.293
Ian Desmond	86	145	86	94	20	11	.265
Rougned Odor	87	155	80	85	29	13	.270
Matt Carpenter	89	145	94	83	29	3	.284
Wil Myers	90	135	84	78	25	17	.258
Mike Napoli	92	145	81	89	32	4	.263
A. Rendon	95	135	80	79	20	11	.280
Jarrod Dyson	96	120	86	56	3	43	.255
Evan Longoria	97	160	80	86	27	2	.274
Billy Hamilton	98	115	82	47	4	53	.233
Aledmys Diaz	99	135	96	81	19	3	.302
J. Lucroy	101	135	69	72	21	4	.289
S. Piscotty	102	150	84	95	16	5	.283
Miguel Sano	107	125	75	88	27	1	.279
Jason Kipnis	109	145	88	67	27	9	.284
A. Benintendi	110	155	97	84	7	6	.299
D. Swanson	113	158	94	77	9	16	.289
Y. Tomas	115	135	74	90	25	1	.282
Dexter Fowler	117	150	101	58	21	10	.270
David Dahl	120	150	94	74	8	14	.285
E. Nunez	121	145	69	68	13	24	.275

Hitter	Ovr	G	R	RBI	HR	SB	BA
G. Polanco	122	145	82	80	22	11	.258
Eugenio Suarez	123	155	71	67	25	11	.275
Victor Martinez	125	135	74	95	23	0	.291
Eric Hosmer	129	145	81	90	17	6	.285
Alex Bregman	132	145	77	86	16	6	.284
Jake Lamb	134	140	87	70	21	6	.274
Lorenzo Cain	137	125	81	77	12	8	.299
Adam Duvall	140	145	76	82	32	5	.242
C. Dickerson	141	120	69	82	20	2	.300
K. Morales	145	150	77	96	23	0	.274
Hanley Ramirez	149	130	78	87	20	5	.277
Russell Martin	150	125	67	79	19	3	.267
Salvador Perez	151	130	64	75	27	0	.259
Jay Bruce	154	140	75	88	26	6	.242
K. Kiermaier	156	140	79	57	23	14	.260
Ryon Healy	157	145	81	85	13	0	.292
T. Tulowitzki	158	130	76	82	21	2	.293
Jorge Soler	162	145	67	82	25	0	.278
Marcell Ozuna	166	150	72	83	21	2	.275
David Peralta	167	125	75	82	14	3	.294
C. Granderson	169	145	89	68	23	6	.252
Tom Murphy	170	80	60	77	14	7	.275
Melky Cabrera	172	145	75	85	14	2	.288
J. Bradley Jr.	173	135	80	76	21	7	.254
Brandon Belt	176	140	86	75	16	5	.280
B. Crawford	180	150	71	89	22	5	.265
Dustin Pedroia	181	140	94	66	9	8	.300
Maikel Franco	182	155	74	85	24	3	.248
Hunter Pence	183	115	74	82	15	4	.281

Top 500 Player Projections

Hitter	Ovr	G	R	RBI	HR	SB	BA
Jung Ho Kang	185	100	68	88	19	3	.265
Byron Buxton	187	145	59	64	11	28	.256
Logan Forsythe	189	140	85	61	24	8	.269
Y. Grandal	197	125	63	77	22	0	.249
Shin-Soo Choo	201	110	78	62	15	11	.272
Denard Span	202	135	87	53	6	15	.285
Brian McCann	203	130	71	85	16	2	.238
Stephen Vogt	204	125	71	72	17	0	.260
A. Russell	206	150	75	100	19	5	.247
Ben Zobrist	208	125	83	80	15	6	.277
Martin Prado	209	150	80	73	7	4	.292
M. Moustakas	212	130	75	73	21	2	.261
M. Saunders	213	140	69	71	22	0	.278
Brad Miller	214	150	77	68	22	9	.259
Joc Pederson	215	135	69	73	23	6	.250
Nomar Mazara	217	155	64	69	25	0	.276
Neil Walker	218	140	71	80	20	3	.281
Chris Carter	220	100	68	82	26	2	.247
Marcus Semien	224	155	70	70	27	7	.251
Jacoby Ellsbury	231	125	78	64	6	18	.261
Starlin Castro	234	150	66	76	22	4	.276
Jayson Werth	235	140	76	73	18	4	.257
Josh Bell	237	145	87	78	7	0	.293
Jose Ramirez	239	150	77	64	10	13	.260
Randal Grichuk	240	125	62	57	19	5	.291
Yadier Molina	241	130	61	74	5	3	.287
Jose Peraza	242	135	49	54	3	33	.289
Brett Gardner	243	145	92	61	9	11	.256
J.T. Realmuto	244	125	58	55	10	9	.279

Hitter	Ovr	G	R	RBI	HR	SB	BA
Matt Holliday	245	120	70	85	16	0	.278
T. Jankowski	246	120	72	39	3	34	.255
N. Castellanos	249	130	61	73	16	2	.283
Ender Inciarte	251	125	86	49	5	12	.285
Tim Anderson	252	145	81	59	7	14	.280
W. Contreras	256	110	60	65	8	2	.293
Josh Reddick	259	125	64	67	17	5	.273
A. Cabrera	261	145	67	64	23	4	.271
Trevor Plouffe	262	145	63	74	21	2	.257
M. Brantley	263	100	63	74	14	2	.288
Scott Schebler	264	145	74	88	8	2	.269
Justin Bour	266	135	62	77	20	0	.277
Nick Markakis	267	155	70	72	10	2	.286
Brandon Moss	271	135	63	66	23	2	.260
Orlando Arcia	272	140	79	58	5	25	.251
Max Kepler	275	145	74	87	11	7	.238
C. Hernandez	280	155	84	47	6	20	.268
Yunel Escobar	282	130	74	52	8	4	.294
W. Castillo	283	110	51	64	14	2	.265
Didi Gregorius	284	155	67	65	22	5	.257
J. Schoop	285	140	68	71	23	3	.256
Matt Duffy	286	130	63	69	12	9	.275
Kevin Pillar	287	150	68	53	9	13	.269
Keon Broxton	289	100	37	47	6	36	.246
Derek Norris	290	125	58	59	10	5	.260
Luis Valbuena	293	120	64	65	19	2	.251
Jason Heyward	294	140	69	65	10	7	.263
Travis Shaw	295	90	52	57	21	3	.271
Y. Solarte	296	110	65	73	10	1	.275

Top 500 Player Projections

Hitter	Ovr	G	R	RBI	HR	SB	BA
Alex Gordon	299	120	63	64	10	5	.278
Seth Smith	301	110	76	64	14	0	.258
Brandon Drury	302	135	67	66	18	1	.248
Josh Harrison	303	115	82	56	0	12	.292
Yasiel Puig	305	110	58	59	14	6	.270
Joe Mauer	308	130	77	75	6	2	.270
Chris Owings	309	120	59	55	7	22	.255
Tommy Joseph	311	140	67	70	14	1	.265
Lucas Duda	313	125	60	69	23	0	.246
Carlos Gomez	319	100	74	59	0	10	.275
A.Escobar	322	155	82	59	5	11	.259
Leonys Martin	325	135	61	49	12	12	.254
F.Cervelli	326	100	54	51	4	4	.285
Elvis Andrus	328	145	66	55	6	13	.272
Dom. Santana	329	100	59	66	11	1	.273
James McCann	331	110	45	59	11	0	.267
Matt Joyce	336	135	68	70	16	2	.228
Colby Rasmus	338	100	53	58	19	3	.248
Eric Thames	341	130	63	78	15	0	.245
Lo. Chisenhall	345	120	58	64	9	4	.266
Devon Travis	349	80	71	54	8	3	.301
M. Conforto	350	80	53	63	14	1	.264
Freddy Galvis	351	155	58	56	21	10	.233
Tyler Flowers	360	100	43	51	9	0	.280
Joe Panik	362	135	67	56	8	4	.284
John Jaso	377	90	71	55	9	0	.275
M. Moreland	381	100	53	61	14	1	.269
Jedd Gyorko	385	110	57	65	20	0	.247
Chase Headley	391	125	58	54	8	5	.258

Hitter	Ovr	G	R	RBI	HR	SB	BA
Tyler Naquin	396	100	58	51	6	5	.276
Avisail Garcia	406	100	52	54	9	5	.264
Cody Asche	416	110	51	52	10	5	.248
R. Zimmerman	423	100	53	62	11	3	.253
H. Kendrick	430	80	63	51	5	6	.285
Mike Zunino	444	45	43	51	9	0	.223
Tony Wolters	452	80	36	57	2	5	.250
Alex Dickerson	456	80	51	53	5	5	.261
B. Phillips	457	80	50	51	4	10	.284
L. Morrison	458	125	53	53	12	5	.244
Jarrett Parker	460	125	46	52	14	0	.255
Cameron Rupp	467	80	40	46	8	1	.245
Yan Gomes	468	70	43	49	8	0	.234
Jordy Mercer	476	145	59	57	12	1	.249
Kolten Wong	477	110	58	55	10	5	.249
David Wright	479	40	52	42	3	3	.309
Peter O'Brien	481	90	35	63	15	0	.245
E. Carrera	485	90	57	40	4	6	.263
A. Simmons	488	145	55	51	5	7	.260
Byung-ho Park	490	50	57	64	5	1	.233
Yulieski Gurriel	498	120	54	57	0	2	.261

Top 500 Player Projections

Hitter projections conclude with per-game statistics for the four categories most often represented by 'counting numbers.' Players included are projected to appear in at least 75 games in 2017. Here are the top 25 hitters, sorted by runs-per-game:

Hitter	Ovr	H Rank	R	G	R/G
Devon Travis	349	190	71	80	0.89
A.J. Pollock	9	8	103	130	0.79
John Jaso	377	195	71	90	0.79
Howie Kendrick	430	203	63	80	0.79
Charlie Blackmon	10	9	108	140	0.77
Kyle Schwarber	32	26	105	140	0.75
Tom Murphy	170	104	60	80	0.75
Carlos Gomez	319	179	74	100	0.74
Jarrod Dyson	96	69	86	120	0.72
Billy Hamilton	98	71	82	115	0.71
Josh Harrison	303	173	82	115	0.71
Aledmys Diaz	99	72	96	135	0.71
Shin-Soo Choo	201	116	78	110	0.71
Kris Bryant	6	5	112	158	0.71
DJ LeMahieu	83	60	106	150	0.71
Trea Turner	21	19	102	145	0.70
Seth Smith	301	171	76	110	0.69
Ender Inciarte	251	144	86	125	0.69
Nolan Arenado	3	3	108	158	0.68
Jung Ho Kang	185	112	68	100	0.68
Chris Carter	220	129	68	100	0.68
Josh Donaldson	7	6	107	158	0.68
Dexter Fowler	117	80	101	150	0.67
Dustin Pedroia	181	109	94	140	0.67
Ian Kinsler	22	20	104	155	0.67

Diamond Dividends: Creative Strategies to Profit Through Fantasy Baseball

Here are the top 25 hitters, sorted by runs-batted-in-per-game:

Hitter	Ovr	H Rank	RBI	G	RBI/G
Tom Murphy	170	104	77	80	0.96
Jung Ho Kang	185	112	88	100	0.88
Chris Carter	220	129	82	100	0.82
Michael Conforto	350	191	63	80	0.79
Gary Sanchez	36	29	98	130	0.75
Giancarlo Stanton	33	27	101	135	0.75
Carlos Gonzalez	29	24	108	145	0.74
Michael Brantley	263	150	74	100	0.74
E. Encarnacion	58	44	111	150	0.74
Nolan Arenado	3	3	116	158	0.73
Nelson Cruz	13	12	99	135	0.73
Hunter Pence	183	111	82	115	0.71
Tony Wolters	452	205	57	80	0.71
Matt Holliday	245	141	85	120	0.71
Miguel Sano	107	75	88	125	0.70
Victor Martinez	125	85	95	135	0.70
Peter O'Brien	481	215	63	90	0.70
Corey Dickerson	141	91	82	120	0.68
Devon Travis	349	190	54	80	0.68
Miguel Cabrera	15	13	101	150	0.67
Hanley Ramirez	149	93	87	130	0.67
Jose Bautista	24	22	100	150	0.67
Yasmany Tomas	115	79	90	135	0.67
Addison Russell	206	120	100	150	0.67
Yangervis Solarte	296	169	73	110	0.66

Top 500 Player Projections

Here are the top 25 hitters, sorted by home-runs-per-game:

Hitter	Ovr	H Rank	HR	G	HR/G
Brian Dozier	19	17	50	157	0.32
Nelson Cruz	13	12	38	135	0.28
Josh Donaldson	7	6	44	158	0.28
Kris Bryant	6	5	42	158	0.27
Todd Frazier	44	35	41	155	0.26
Chris Carter	220	129	26	100	0.26
Jose Bautista	24	22	39	150	0.26
Albert Pujols	63	48	39	150	0.26
Giancarlo Stanton	33	27	35	135	0.26
Mark Trumbo	60	46	37	145	0.26
Khris Davis	39	32	38	150	0.25
Chris Davis	37	30	39	155	0.25
Nolan Arenado	3	3	38	158	0.24
Bryce Harper	12	11	33	140	0.24
Travis Shaw	295	168	21	90	0.23
Carlos Santana	78	56	36	158	0.23
J.D. Martinez	17	15	31	140	0.22
Mike Napoli	92	67	32	145	0.22
Adam Duvall	140	90	32	145	0.22
Mike Trout	1	1	35	159	0.22
Yoenis Cespedes	25	23	33	150	0.22
Miguel Sano	107	75	27	125	0.22
Mookie Betts	2	2	34	158	0.22
Trevor Story	52	40	32	150	0.21
Salvador Perez	151	95	27	130	0.21

Diamond Dividends: Creative Strategies to Profit Through Fantasy Baseball

Here are the top 25 hitters, sorted by stolen-bases-per-game:

Hitter	Ovr	H Rank	SB	G	SB/G
Billy Hamilton	98	71	53	115	0.46
Keon Broxton	289	164	36	100	0.36
Jarrod Dyson	96	69	43	120	0.36
Jonathan Villar	30	25	46	130	0.35
Dee Gordon	42	33	53	150	0.35
A.J. Pollock	9	8	44	130	0.34
Travis Jankowski	246	142	34	120	0.28
Rajai Davis	84	61	37	135	0.27
Jose Peraza	242	138	33	135	0.24
Starling Marte	8	7	35	150	0.23
Trea Turner	21	19	31	145	0.21
Jean Segura	59	45	31	150	0.21
Jose Altuve	11	10	32	159	0.20
Byron Buxton	187	113	28	145	0.19
Chris Owings	309	176	22	120	0.18
Orlando Arcia	272	155	25	140	0.18
Eduardo Nunez	121	82	24	145	0.17
Mike Trout	1	1	24	159	0.15
Charlie Blackmon	10	9	21	140	0.15
Jacoby Ellsbury	231	131	18	125	0.14
Odubel Herrera	48	39	23	160	0.14
Mookie Betts	2	2	21	158	0.13
Cesar Hernandez	280	157	20	155	0.13
Paul Goldschmidt	5	4	20	158	0.13
Wil Myers	90	66	17	135	0.13

Top 500 Player Projections

Here are the 2017 fantasy baseball statistical projections for the pitchers who appeared in the top 500 players – the 'Ovr' column refers to the player's overall ranking, including all positions:

Pitcher	Ovr	W	K	ERA	WHIP	SV
Clayton Kershaw	4	21	236	1.92	0.808	0
Max Scherzer	14	18	278	3.25	1.022	0
Jake Arrieta	26	20	200	2.92	1.011	0
Johnny Cueto	27	19	209	2.81	1.066	0
Chris Sale	28	19	239	3.34	1.040	0
Corey Kluber	31	18	247	3.30	1.072	0
M. Bumgarner	34	17	241	3.27	1.045	0
Noah Syndergaard	40	17	237	2.93	1.107	0
Jon Lester	41	19	208	3.13	1.067	0
Wade Davis	49	3	71	1.53	0.964	66
Stephen Strasburg	50	17	240	3.33	1.108	0
Aaron Sanchez	51	21	159	2.83	1.087	0
Kyle Hendricks	55	19	170	2.96	1.054	0
Zach Britton	56	4	74	1.02	0.913	54
David Price	62	18	242	3.71	1.135	0
Aroldis Chapman	69	3	98	1.63	0.932	52
Seung Hwan Oh	71	3	102	2.06	0.947	49
Carlos Carrasco	72	17	207	3.48	1.092	0
Jacob deGrom	73	16	197	2.98	1.130	0
Kenley Jansen	74	3	94	2.09	0.828	50
Mark Melancon	75	3	66	1.82	0.910	54
Steven Matz	77	18	176	2.54	1.216	0
Rich Hill	81	15	187	3.22	1.009	0
John Lackey	88	19	180	3.51	1.154	0
Drew Pomeranz	91	17	208	3.61	1.179	0

Pitcher	Ovr	W	K	ERA	WHIP	SV
Marco Estrada	93	18	174	3.56	1.141	0
Masahiro Tanaka	94	17	155	3.41	1.062	0
Justin Verlander	100	16	220	4.08	1.140	0
Danny Duffy	103	16	189	3.71	1.130	0
Cole Hamels	104	17	207	3.61	1.239	0
Cody Allen	105	3	90	2.58	1.077	47
Tanner Roark	106	18	156	3.23	1.193	0
Kenta Maeda	108	15	199	3.68	1.146	0
Zack Greinke	111	17	166	3.50	1.147	0
Roberto Osuna	112	3	79	2.66	0.942	44
Edwin Diaz	114	3	87	2.59	1.118	49
Julio Teheran	116	16	173	3.59	1.138	0
Craig Kimbrel	118	3	90	2.97	1.048	47
Yu Darvish	119	14	195	3.34	1.170	0
Michael Fulmer	124	17	157	3.61	1.145	0
Jeurys Familia	126	3	82	2.33	1.154	44
Michael Pineda	127	15	210	4.02	1.174	0
Rick Porcello	128	17	174	3.87	1.162	0
Kelvin Herrera	130	3	76	2.57	1.040	43
Dallas Keuchel	131	17	168	3.68	1.193	0
Felix Hernandez	133	17	158	3.50	1.196	0
Danny Salazar	135	16	213	3.77	1.293	0
Drew Smyly	136	17	190	3.96	1.220	0
Matt Shoemaker	138	15	169	3.51	1.192	0
Chris Devenski	139	13	123	3.16	0.938	0
Tony Watson	142	3	64	2.59	1.062	43
Alex Colome	143	3	95	2.25	1.127	35
Lance McCullers	144	15	212	3.26	1.392	0
Jerad Eickhoff	146	13	177	3.71	1.138	0

Pitcher	Ovr	W	K	ERA	WHIP	SV
Carlos Martinez	147	16	184	3.51	1.295	0
Jose Quintana	148	15	180	3.73	1.212	0
Hisashi Iwakuma	152	16	159	3.85	1.185	0
Jeff Samardzija	153	15	180	3.97	1.191	0
J.A. Happ	155	16	169	3.75	1.245	0
Ian Kennedy	159	13	194	3.77	1.230	0
Alex Wood	160	14	153	3.19	1.246	0
Chris Archer	161	12	231	4.25	1.228	0
Junior Guerra	163	14	141	3.41	1.176	0
Ken Giles	164	2	89	3.17	1.132	40
Collin McHugh	165	15	193	3.99	1.268	0
Julio Urias	168	15	182	3.20	1.402	0
Jake Odorizzi	171	14	179	3.94	1.217	0
Matt Harvey	174	15	157	3.38	1.298	0
Sam Dyson	175	3	50	2.44	1.232	43
James Paxton	177	16	157	3.73	1.291	0
Gerrit Cole	178	15	148	3.43	1.282	0
Kevin Gausman	179	15	185	4.07	1.273	0
Jameson Taillon	184	14	126	3.67	1.139	0
Joe Ross	186	14	138	3.51	1.222	0
F.Rodriguez	188	3	58	2.96	1.047	36
Scott Kazmir	190	14	175	3.96	1.269	0
Luis Severino	191	15	148	3.29	1.351	0
Sean Manaea	192	14	166	4.12	1.211	0
Cam Bedrosian	193	3	45	1.83	1.317	42
Adam Conley	194	15	168	3.55	1.365	0
Jaime Garcia	195	13	172	4.07	1.209	0
Aaron Nola	196	12	167	3.60	1.259	0
Garrett Richards	198	14	119	3.15	1.240	0

Pitcher	Ovr	W	K	ERA	WHIP	SV
Gio Gonzalez	199	15	192	4.24	1.315	0
Ervin Santana	200	15	166	4.00	1.279	0
A.J. Ramos	205	3	76	2.60	1.239	32
Miguel Gonzalez	207	15	131	3.46	1.302	0
Mike Leake	210	16	138	4.04	1.259	0
Raisel Iglesias	211	2	89	3.39	1.150	31
Daniel Norris	216	14	152	3.76	1.320	0
Lance Lynn	219	12	177	4.01	1.280	0
Trevor Bauer	221	14	181	4.18	1.328	0
Matt Andriese	222	13	146	3.90	1.254	0
Adam Wainwright	223	14	163	4.22	1.268	0
Michael Wacha	225	15	157	4.05	1.332	0
Carlos Rodon	226	14	197	4.20	1.393	0
Francisco Liriano	227	14	203	4.48	1.365	0
Taijuan Walker	228	14	164	4.40	1.268	0
Blake Snell	229	14	197	3.33	1.579	0
Vince Velasquez	230	11	210	4.41	1.316	0
Wei-Yin Chen	232	13	138	3.89	1.255	0
Bartolo Colon	233	14	134	4.12	1.226	0
Robbie Ray	236	13	239	4.65	1.409	0
Ed. Rodriguez	238	14	142	4.05	1.305	0
David Robertson	247	2	80	3.41	1.178	28
Marcus Stroman	248	13	137	4.21	1.238	0
Andrew Miller	250	3	109	1.63	0.770	0
Tyler Chatwood	253	17	139	4.12	1.401	0
Tyler Anderson	254	14	142	4.34	1.292	0
Chris Rusin	255	16	135	4.11	1.374	0
Dellin Betances	257	3	136	2.48	0.993	0
Zach Davies	258	12	160	4.37	1.256	0

Top 500 Player Projections

Pitcher	Ovr	W	K	ERA	WHIP	SV
Ryan Madson	260	2	51	3.37	1.184	32
Jharel Cotton	265	9	93	4.30	0.914	0
Jeremy Hellickson	268	12	164	4.36	1.285	0
Ivan Nova	269	14	145	4.34	1.305	0
David Phelps	270	2	198	3.22	1.273	0
Rubby de la Rosa	273	12	135	3.84	1.364	0
A.DeSclafani	274	12	144	4.33	1.287	0
Jon Gray	276	5	218	4.31	1.271	0
Zack Wheeler	277	13	131	3.87	1.440	0
Fernando Rodney	278	2	70	3.69	1.390	30
R.A. Dickey	279	13	145	4.49	1.298	0
Sonny Gray	281	12	135	4.30	1.310	0
Kendall Graveman	288	14	118	4.15	1.355	0
Charlie Morton	291	10	106	3.69	1.325	0
Matt Moore	292	12	174	4.61	1.375	0
Cody Anderson	297	12	118	4.00	1.398	0
Wade Miley	298	13	162	4.68	1.391	0
Evan Scribner	300	6	40	0.73	0.726	0
Edinson Volquez	304	13	147	4.48	1.404	0
Tyler Duffey	306	13	159	4.75	1.427	0
Jim Johnson	307	2	58	3.91	1.444	26
Will Harris	310	3	71	2.19	1.006	0
Jesse Chavez	312	9	114	4.25	1.325	0
Mike Foltynewicz	314	11	155	4.66	1.408	0
Vidal Nuno	315	8	89	3.71	1.282	0
Neftali Feliz	316	2	44	4.04	1.234	22
Bud Norris	317	11	144	4.54	1.421	0
Brad Brach	318	3	81	2.36	1.123	0
Brandon Maurer	320	2	60	4.16	1.233	19

Diamond Dividends: Creative Strategies to Profit Through Fantasy Baseball

Pitcher	Ovr	W	K	ERA	WHIP	SV
Patrick Corbin	321	13	159	4.76	1.466	0
Tyler Skaggs	323	9	131	4.40	1.387	0
Clay Buchholz	324	11	138	4.80	1.335	0
Pedro Strop	327	3	73	2.79	0.976	0
Joe Smith	330	7	52	3.28	1.150	0
Tyler Glasnow	332	9	116	4.07	1.505	0
Hector Rondon	333	3	66	2.93	1.000	0
Addison Reed	334	3	72	2.61	1.127	0
Luke Gregerson	335	3	68	3.09	1.001	0
Shawn Kelley	337	3	71	2.83	1.047	0
Sergio Romo	339	5	52	2.86	1.045	0
Koji Uehara	340	3	65	3.03	0.940	0
George Kontos	342	6	36	2.51	1.102	0
Justin Grimm	343	6	69	3.53	1.247	0
Tyler Thornburg	344	3	64	2.40	1.070	0
Anibal Sanchez	346	9	159	5.29	1.318	0
Joe Musgrove	347	7	73	4.26	1.225	0
Joaquin Benoit	348	3	60	2.53	1.070	0
Darren O'Day	352	3	66	2.95	1.085	0
Pedro Baez	353	2	72	3.09	1.076	0
Yusmeiro Petit	354	6	72	4.19	1.217	0
Shelby Miller	355	11	108	4.55	1.458	0
Jared Hughes	356	7	36	2.71	1.323	0
Fernando Salas	357	5	62	3.93	1.140	0
Hector Neris	358	2	72	2.78	1.153	0
Carson Smith	359	4	32	0.39	1.195	0
Steve Cishek	361	3	70	3.05	1.200	0
Carlos Frias	363	5	28	1.78	1.091	0
Brad Ziegler	364	3	54	2.31	1.230	0

Top 500 Player Projections

Pitcher	Ovr	W	K	ERA	WHIP	SV
Clayton Richard	365	11	92	3.96	1.514	0
Mike Bolsinger	366	9	106	4.52	1.484	0
Matt Belisle	367	6	34	2.38	1.286	0
Bryan Shaw	368	3	67	3.09	1.213	0
Brad Hand	369	2	103	3.70	1.280	0
Zach Putnam	370	5	47	2.70	1.264	0
Dan Otero	371	3	49	2.93	1.118	0
Pat Neshek	372	2	52	3.05	0.984	0
Juan Nicasio	373	7	116	4.76	1.436	0
Tommy Milone	374	10	111	4.64	1.434	0
Justin Wilson	375	5	65	3.89	1.265	0
Mike Dunn	376	6	51	3.65	1.292	0
Trevor Cahill	378	6	71	3.76	1.411	0
Jeff Locke	379	11	110	4.66	1.435	0
Hunter Strickland	380	2	53	2.99	1.047	0
Santiago Casilla	382	2	61	3.14	1.134	0
Fernando Abad	383	5	45	3.52	1.222	0
Jeff Manship	384	5	34	2.75	1.225	0
Alex Cobb	386	8	86	3.96	1.525	0
Carlos Torres	387	2	74	3.26	1.265	0
Jonathan Broxton	388	5	56	4.13	1.245	0
Tyler Lyons	389	4	47	3.60	1.155	0
Blake Treinen	390	3	54	2.70	1.307	0
Michael Lorenzen	392	2	74	3.30	1.282	0
J.P. Howell	393	5	43	3.21	1.315	0
Jose Alvarez	394	5	55	3.46	1.372	0
Will Smith	395	2	70	3.23	1.262	0
Hansel Robles	397	2	73	3.51	1.245	0
Williams Perez	398	10	76	4.46	1.429	0

Pitcher	Ovr	W	K	ERA	WHIP	SV
Archie Bradley	399	12	175	5.24	1.578	0
Kyle Ryan	400	5	34	3.30	1.247	0
Felipe Rivero	401	2	70	3.87	1.176	0
Luke Weaver	402	6	107	4.70	1.541	0
Seth Maness	403	6	33	3.56	1.305	0
A. Caminero	404	6	58	3.57	1.497	0
Boone Logan	405	4	51	3.80	1.245	0
Jeremy Jeffress	407	3	42	2.47	1.295	0
Brett Cecil	408	2	61	3.41	1.214	0
Kevin Siegrist	409	2	61	3.13	1.275	0
F. Rodriguez	410	4	47	4.14	1.179	0
Jumbo Diaz	411	4	43	3.43	1.289	0
Jake Diekman	412	2	72	3.60	1.317	0
Bryan Morris	413	5	36	2.93	1.436	0
Jose Urena	414	11	110	4.84	1.493	0
Drew Hutchison	415	7	105	5.23	1.408	0
Tony Sipp	417	4	49	4.01	1.278	0
Chris Bassitt	418	8	95	4.34	1.570	0
Jose De Leon	419	7	94	4.35	1.552	0
Josh Fields	420	4	57	4.34	1.324	0
Jason Grilli	421	2	64	3.81	1.265	0
Danny Farquhar	422	2	63	3.53	1.310	0
Luis Avilan	424	3	46	3.58	1.255	0
Antonio Bastardo	425	2	71	4.06	1.279	0
John Axford	426	5	57	4.03	1.481	0
David Hernandez	427	4	57	3.91	1.426	0
Dan Jennings	428	3	42	2.47	1.435	0
Ricky Nolasco	429	9	154	5.31	1.434	0
Liam Hendriks	431	2	56	3.73	1.243	0

Pitcher	Ovr	W	K	ERA	WHIP	SV
Xavier Cedeno	432	2	46	3.48	1.189	0
Oliver Perez	433	4	55	4.50	1.357	0
Jhoulys Chacin	434	10	152	5.60	1.433	0
Junichi Tazawa	435	2	60	4.00	1.253	0
Erasmo Ramirez	436	2	79	3.95	1.319	0
Zach McAllister	437	2	71	3.55	1.415	0
Mike Clevinger	438	6	77	4.76	1.494	0
Joe Kelly	439	2	137	4.13	1.523	0
Blaine Hardy	440	4	34	3.28	1.412	0
Chaz Roe	441	3	41	3.72	1.312	0
Jake McGee	442	2	50	3.80	1.246	0
Reynaldo Lopez	443	6	80	4.61	1.552	0
Trevor Gott	445	3	24	1.75	1.391	0
Drew Storen	446	2	52	4.27	1.184	0
Bruce Rondon	447	2	41	3.44	1.213	0
Ryan Tepera	448	3	23	3.00	1.204	0
K. Quackenbush	449	2	46	3.76	1.249	0
Casey Fien	450	4	46	4.82	1.270	0
Mike Morin	451	3	47	4.69	1.222	0
Trevor Rosenthal	453	2	79	3.71	1.587	0
Aaron Loup	454	3	42	4.65	1.260	0
Tyler Cravy	455	3	28	3.33	1.360	0
Brandon Morrow	459	3	16	2.45	1.370	0
Javier Lopez	461	3	20	3.32	1.308	0
Randall Delgado	462	2	72	4.20	1.433	0
Brian Duensing	463	3	26	4.01	1.277	0
Chasen Shreve	464	3	47	4.83	1.346	0
Erik Goeddel	465	2	34	4.19	1.234	0
Alexi Ogando	466	4	43	3.95	1.576	0

Pitcher	Ovr	W	K	ERA	WHIP	SV
Chad Qualls	469	4	33	4.78	1.363	0
Marc Rzepczynski	470	2	43	3.41	1.493	0
Corey Knebel	471	2	48	4.44	1.378	0
Arodys Vizcaino	472	2	45	3.95	1.472	0
Jose Berrios	473	11	124	4.34	1.856	0
Brad Boxberger	474	2	53	4.23	1.424	0
Keone Kela	475	2	60	5.47	1.304	0
Tommy Kahnle	478	2	41	3.38	1.507	0
Rob Scahill	480	2	25	3.26	1.368	0
Chris Hatcher	482	2	48	4.80	1.359	0
Matt Barnes	483	2	56	4.28	1.473	0
Justin Miller	484	3	41	5.43	1.397	0
Daniel Hudson	486	2	63	4.99	1.393	0
Andrew Chafin	487	3	55	6.09	1.346	0
Ryan Webb	489	3	25	4.52	1.417	0
Jeanmar Gomez	491	2	46	4.18	1.431	0
Bo Schultz	492	2	19	5.19	1.189	0
Kyle Lobstein	493	3	25	4.50	1.459	0
Tom Wilhelmsen	494	4	44	5.33	1.444	0
Matt Thornton	495	2	18	4.40	1.357	0
Scott Oberg	496	3	32	5.17	1.473	0
Jake Petricka	497	3	36	4.09	1.697	0
Tony Cingrani	499	2	46	4.57	1.531	0
Shawn Tolleson	500	3	52	5.89	1.414	0

Top 500 Player Projections

Similarly to hitters, pitchers have their own per-unit value, however, it is largely confined to only *one* statistic: strikeouts-per-inning-pitched. Here are 100 starting pitchers, sorted by strikeouts-per-inning, with a minimum of 15 projected starts for 2017:

Pitcher	Ovr	P Rank	GS	IP	W	K/IP
Yu Darvish	119	39	25	150	14	1.30
Lance McCullers	144	53	27	171	15	1.24
Max Scherzer	14	2	33	228	18	1.22
S. Strasburg	50	11	30	197	17	1.22
Clayton Kershaw	4	1	33	199	21	1.19
Robbie Ray	236	103	31	204	13	1.17
Rich Hill	81	23	27	160	15	1.17
N. Syndergaard	40	8	31	203	17	1.17
Vince Velasquez	230	100	30	181	11	1.16
Danny Salazar	135	47	31	187	16	1.14
Chris Archer	161	62	32	207	12	1.12
Chris Sale	28	5	33	217	19	1.10
Jon Gray	276	120	33	198	5	1.10
Blake Snell	229	99	30	179	14	1.10
Julio Urias	168	66	28	167	15	1.09
M. Bumgarner	34	7	33	222	17	1.09
Corey Kluber	31	6	33	229	18	1.08
Michael Pineda	127	42	32	195	15	1.08
Juan Nicasio	373	179	18	108	7	1.07
Carlos Carrasco	72	18	31	196	17	1.06
Francisco Liriano	227	97	32	193	14	1.05
Drew Pomeranz	91	25	31	200	17	1.04
Aaron Nola	196	82	27	161	12	1.04

Pitcher	Ovr	P Rank	GS	IP	W	K/IP
Tyler Glasnow	332	147	19	113	9	1.03
Kenta Maeda	108	33	32	195	15	1.02
Alex Wood	160	61	25	150	14	1.02
Justin Verlander	100	28	33	217	16	1.01
David Price	62	15	34	239	18	1.01
Carlos Rodon	226	96	33	195	14	1.01
Cole Hamels	104	30	32	208	17	1.00
Jacob deGrom	73	19	30	198	16	0.99
Charlie Morton	291	126	18	107	10	0.99
Jake Arrieta	26	3	31	202	20	0.99
Jon Lester	41	9	32	212	19	0.98
Gio Gonzalez	199	84	32	197	15	0.97
Drew Smyly	136	48	33	195	17	0.97
Ian Kennedy	159	60	31	200	13	0.97
Steven Matz	77	22	30	182	18	0.97
Rubby de la Rosa	273	118	23	140	12	0.96
Chris Devenski	139	50	21	128	13	0.96
Garrett Richards	198	83	25	124	14	0.96
Daniel Norris	216	90	27	159	14	0.96
Danny Duffy	103	29	30	199	16	0.95
Collin McHugh	165	65	31	204	15	0.95
Tyler Skaggs	323	143	23	139	9	0.94
Scott Kazmir	190	76	31	186	14	0.94
Lance Lynn	219	91	32	189	12	0.94
Kevin Gausman	179	72	33	199	15	0.93
Jesse Chavez	312	135	21	123	9	0.93
Drew Hutchison	415	215	19	114	7	0.92
Carlos Martinez	147	55	31	200	16	0.92
Luis Severino	191	77	27	161	15	0.92

Top 500 Player Projections

Pitcher	Ovr	P Rank	GS	IP	W	K/IP
James Paxton	177	70	29	171	16	0.92
Adam Conley	194	80	31	183	15	0.92
Archie Bradley	399	200	32	191	12	0.92
John Lackey	88	24	33	198	19	0.91
Jake Odorizzi	171	67	33	197	14	0.91
Mike Bolsinger	366	172	20	117	9	0.91
Trevor Bauer	221	92	31	200	14	0.91
Johnny Cueto	27	4	33	231	19	0.90
E. Rodriguez	238	104	26	157	14	0.90
M. Foltynewicz	314	136	29	173	11	0.90
Gerrit Cole	178	71	28	166	15	0.89
Taijuan Walker	228	98	31	184	14	0.89
Joe Ross	186	74	26	155	14	0.89
Matt Shoemaker	138	49	32	190	15	0.89
Marco Estrada	93	26	33	196	18	0.89
Bud Norris	317	139	27	163	11	0.88
Zack Greinke	111	34	31	188	17	0.88
Jose De Leon	419	218	18	107	7	0.88
Jerad Eickhoff	146	54	31	202	13	0.88
Masahiro Tanaka	94	27	30	177	17	0.88
Julio Teheran	116	37	33	198	16	0.87
Jose Quintana	148	56	32	207	15	0.87
Tyler Duffey	306	132	31	183	13	0.87
Anibal Sanchez	346	157	25	183	9	0.87
Tyler Anderson	254	109	27	164	14	0.87
Vidal Nuno	315	137	17	103	8	0.86
Felix Hernandez	133	46	31	183	17	0.86
Matt Harvey	174	68	30	182	15	0.86
Patrick Corbin	321	142	31	185	13	0.86

Pitcher	Ovr	P Rank	GS	IP	W	K/IP
Matt Moore	292	127	31	203	12	0.86
Jaime Garcia	195	81	30	201	13	0.86
Sean Manaea	192	78	32	194	14	0.86
Kyle Hendricks	55	13	31	200	19	0.85
Dallas Keuchel	131	45	33	198	17	0.85
J.A. Happ	155	59	31	200	16	0.85
Jose Berrios	473	262	25	148	11	0.84
Michael Wacha	225	95	31	188	15	0.84
A. DeSclafani	274	119	29	173	12	0.83
Michael Fulmer	124	40	32	189	17	0.83
Jeff Samardzija	153	58	33	217	15	0.83
Zach Davies	258	112	32	193	12	0.83
Wade Miley	298	129	33	196	13	0.83
Ervin Santana	200	85	31	201	15	0.83
Matt Andriese	222	93	30	177	13	0.82
Junior Guerra	163	63	29	171	14	0.82
J. Hellickson	268	115	33	199	12	0.82
Marcus Stroman	248	106	28	167	13	0.82
Jameson Taillon	184	73	26	154	14	0.82
Yu Darvish	119	39	25	150	14	1.30

Finally, here are the top 75 relief pitchers, sorted by strikeouts-per-inning:

Pitcher	Ovr	P Rank	SV	K	IP	K/IP
Edwin Diaz	114	36	49	87	51	1.71
Aroldis Chapman	69	16	52	98	59	1.66
Dellin Betances	257	111	0	136	82	1.66
Andrew Miller	250	107	0	109	66	1.65
Craig Kimbrel	118	38	47	90	58	1.55
Kenley Jansen	74	20	50	94	62	1.52
Ken Giles	164	64	40	89	60	1.48
Shawn Kelley	337	151	0	71	53	1.34
Trevor Rosenthal	453	248	0	79	59	1.34
Jason Grilli	421	220	0	64	49	1.31
Cody Allen	105	31	47	90	69	1.30
Koji Uehara	340	153	0	65	50	1.30
Seung Hwan Oh	71	17	49	102	79	1.29
Keone Kela	475	264	0	60	47	1.28
Brett Cecil	408	208	0	61	48	1.27
David Robertson	247	105	28	80	63	1.27
Tyler Thornburg	344	156	0	64	51	1.25
Will Smith	395	197	0	70	56	1.25
Arodys Vizcaino	472	261	0	45	36	1.25
Pedro Strop	327	145	0	73	59	1.24
Cam Bedrosian	193	79	42	45	37	1.22
Danny Farquhar	422	221	0	63	52	1.21
Bruce Rondon	447	243	0	41	34	1.21
Darren O'Day	352	160	0	66	55	1.20
Hector Neris	358	166	0	72	60	1.20
Jake Diekman	412	212	0	72	61	1.18

Pitcher	Ovr	P Rank	SV	K	IP	K/IP
Corey Knebel	471	260	0	48	41	1.17
Wade Davis	49	10	66	71	61	1.16
A.J. Ramos	205	86	32	76	66	1.15
Steve Cishek	361	168	0	70	61	1.15
Alex Colome	143	52	35	95	83	1.14
Pedro Baez	353	161	0	72	63	1.14
A. Bastardo	425	223	0	71	63	1.13
David Phelps	270	117	0	198	176	1.13
Addison Reed	334	149	0	72	64	1.13
Felipe Rivero	401	202	0	70	63	1.11
Brad Brach	318	140	0	81	73	1.11
Kevin Siegrist	409	209	0	61	55	1.11
Hansel Robles	397	198	0	73	66	1.11
Roberto Osuna	112	35	44	79	72	1.10
F. Rodney	278	122	30	70	64	1.09
Kelvin Herrera	130	44	43	76	70	1.09
Hector Rondon	333	148	0	66	61	1.08
Luke Gregerson	335	150	0	68	63	1.08
Zach Britton	56	14	54	74	69	1.07
Raisel Iglesias	211	89	31	89	83	1.07
Joaquin Benoit	348	159	0	60	56	1.07
Chris Hatcher	482	267	0	48	45	1.07
Jeurys Familia	126	41	44	82	77	1.06
Brad Boxberger	474	263	0	53	50	1.06
Joe Kelly	439	236	0	137	130	1.05
Junichi Tazawa	435	232	0	60	57	1.05
Santiago Casilla	382	186	0	61	58	1.05
Brad Hand	369	175	0	103	98	1.05
Xavier Cedeno	432	229	0	46	44	1.05

Top 500 Player Projections

Pitcher	Ovr	P Rank	SV	K	IP	K/IP
Will Harris	310	134	0	71	68	1.04
Liam Hendriks	431	228	0	56	54	1.04
Zach McAllister	437	234	0	71	69	1.03
Matt Barnes	483	268	0	56	55	1.02
Neftali Feliz	316	138	22	44	44	1.00
Erik Goeddel	465	256	0	34	34	1.00
M. Rzepczynski	470	259	0	43	43	1.00
Daniel Hudson	486	270	0	63	64	0.98
Jake McGee	442	239	0	50	51	0.98
Bryan Shaw	368	174	0	67	69	0.97
Drew Storen	446	242	0	52	54	0.96
Randall Delgado	462	253	0	72	75	0.96
Tommy Kahnle	478	265	0	41	43	0.95
Brandon Maurer	320	141	19	60	63	0.95
Franc. Rodriguez	188	75	36	58	61	0.95
Jim Johnson	307	133	26	58	61	0.95
H. Strickland	380	185	0	53	56	0.95
Carlos Torres	387	190	0	74	79	0.94
Pat Neshek	372	178	0	52	56	0.93
Mark Melancon	75	21	54	66	73	0.90
Edwin Diaz	114	36	49	87	51	1.71
Aroldis Chapman	69	16	52	98	59	1.66
Dellin Betances	257	111	0	136	82	1.66

APPENDIX II –ADDITIONAL ACCESS

By purchasing this book, you will receive a full one-month free trial at Sporfolio. In order to redeem this, please take the following steps:

- Send an email to contact@sporfolio.com with "Diamond Dividends" in the subject line.
- Include some proof-of-purchase in the email. This can be the picture or screenshot of a receipt or confirmation. If you can't produce one, just email us anyway we will do our best to accommodate your request.
- Follow the directions in the email you will receive shortly thereafter.

This one-month free trial will grant you access to everything available to Sporfolio's subscribers, including the Kindle version of this book at no additional cost.

Additional Access

For any questions or comments about anything covered in this book, please feel free to email me at the aforementioned address – contact@sporfolio.com – and I will do my best to respond. I can also be reached on Twitter via the handle @MarioMergola, and it is the social media platform on which I am the most responsive.

Much of what was covered in this book can be utilized for all fantasy sports and is not limited to baseball. Please feel free to experiment with some of the methods covered in this pages and send over some results. I would love to see these strategies in action.

If you have the time, please review *Diamond Dividends: Creative Strategies to Profit Through Fantasy Baseball* on Amazon, Goodreads, and any other website where it applies.

Thank you so much for reading my work. I had a blast writing and assembling this book and I sincerely hope that you enjoyed it. I wish you the best of luck in your future fantasy sports endeavors!

ABOUT THE AUTHOR

Nearly every conversation with Mario Mergola eventually turns to sports. It is for this reason that his family and friends always knew he would continue pursuing this passion as a career. He did not, however, discover his love for writing until his freshman year of college, and he has a few friends and the woman who became his wife to thank for the support and encouragement along the way. Since then, Mergola has worked at ESPN Radio, written for XN Sports, finished 2014 and 2015 with the most correct NFL picks against the spread among experts tracked by NFLPickwatch.com and, most recently, created Sporfolio, found at: https://www.sporfolio.com

Mergola lives in New Jersey with his wife and two children, and he is a self-proclaimed 'lunatic fan' of the New York Yankees, New York Jets, New Jersey Devils, and Brooklyn Nets. He does, however acknowledge that his love for each *sport* will always be greater than the love for his teams.

Especially baseball.

www.ingramcontent.com/pod-product-compliance
Lightning Source LLC
Chambersburg PA
CBHW031406040426
42444CB00005B/435